Page 178

ONCE UPON A RHYME

IMAGINATION FOR A NEW GENERATION

London Vol II
Edited by Steve Twelvetree

Young Writers

First published in Great Britain in 2004 by:
Young Writers
Remus House
Coltsfoot Drive
Peterborough
PE2 9JX
Telephone: 01733 890066
Website: www.youngwriters.co.uk

All Rights Reserved

© Copyright Contributors 2004

SB ISBN 1 84460 540 X

Foreword

Young Writers was established in 1991 and has been passionately devoted to the promotion of reading and writing in children and young adults ever since. The quest continues today. Young Writers remains as committed to engendering the fostering of burgeoning poetic and literary talent as ever.

This year's Young Writers competition has proven as vibrant and dynamic as ever and we are delighted to present a showcase of the best poetry from across the UK. Each poem has been carefully selected from a wealth of *Once Upon A Rhyme* entries before ultimately being published in this, our twelfth primary school poetry series.

Once again, we have been supremely impressed by the overall high quality of the entries we have received. The imagination, energy and creativity which has gone into each young writer's entry made choosing the best poems a challenging and often difficult but ultimately hugely rewarding task - the general high standard of the work submitted amply vindicating this opportunity to bring their poetry to a larger appreciative audience.

We sincerely hope you are pleased with our final selection and that you will enjoy *Once Upon A Rhyme London Vol II* for many years to come.

Contents

Latymer All Saints Primary School
Jack Day (10)	1
Charlotte Wilson (11)	1
Andre Malik (11)	2
Isaac Verissimo (10)	2
Tolu Olufemi (11)	3
Lawrence Ife (10)	3
Priscilla Boateng (10)	4
Charlie Cook (10)	4
Stephanie Christos (10)	5
Corrine Brown (11)	5
Sheniqua Angus (11)	6
Oluwaseun-Mae Adeneye (10)	6
Alice Suker (11)	7
Malachi Dubarry (11)	7

Loughborough Primary School
Roqeeb Ajibola (8)	8
Keani Kerr (7)	8
Michaela Bowley (8)	9
Dean Robinson (7)	9
Morolayo Olatunde (8)	10
Rashorn Evans (8)	10
Leah Williams (10)	11
Leann Byrne (9)	11
Farhia Elmi (9)	12
Zam Zam Aden (9)	12
Abdirahim Ali (10)	13
Ruqayya Smith (10)	13
Rochelle Fraser (10)	14
Khadijah Conroy (9)	14
Ajibola Amire (9)	15
David O'Brien (10)	15
Melika Williams (9)	15
Nicole Voss (9)	16
Ajibike Sobogun (9)	16
Zachariah Ouazene (9)	16
Jerlando Watson (9)	17
Sashkia Myers (10)	17

Daniel Kusimo (10)	17
Nabiel Hafez (9)	18
Sharona Brown (9)	18
Owen Barrett (10)	18
Ben McCormack (9)	19
Kane Nosworthy (8)	19
Rachel Ogunkoya (9)	19
Imran Hussain (9)	20
Desré Denton-Ashley (8)	20
Deborah Adelabu (9)	20
Natalie Robertson (9)	21
Francisco Norena-Gallego (10)	21
Danielle Crawford-Gartell (9)	21
Mariam Elmi (9)	22
Isabel Ribeiro (9)	22
Jason Appeagyei-Boachie (9)	23
Ebtihal Saleh (9)	23
Azharul Islam	24
Merve Etem (8)	24
Regina Okeke (9)	24
Jadian Effik (8)	25

Reay Primary School

Ophelia Gibson Best (10)	25
Hester Carter (10)	26
Luke Wallace-Worrell (7)	26
Clara Hallifax (11)	27
Sarah Agui (7)	27
Lauren Burrows (10)	28
Alysha-Rae Weekes (8)	28
Karim Boustani (9)	29
George Hodgkinson (7)	29
Georgia Whitaker-Hughes (10)	30
Constance Egbemhenghe (8)	30
Esavon Petersen (10)	31
Lily Paine (8)	31
Alice Hirst (10)	32
Dean Bright (11)	33
Erick Hinds (10)	34
Miles Millward (11)	34
Jon Dartnell (9)	35

Jessica Kelly (10)	35
Sophie Hale (10)	36
Beatrice Chamberlain-Kent (7)	36
Lola Meghoma (10)	37
Omari Okwulu (10)	37
Sophia Nesro (11)	38
Oscar Rainbird-Chill (8)	38
Joe Knight (8)	39
Joseph Duggan (7)	39
Nina Carter (8)	40
Taylor Loring (9)	40
Martha Dillon (8)	41
Titan Fiennes Tiffin (8)	42
Kazden Farruggio (9)	42
Ella Morphet (7)	43
Ellen Cullen (8)	43
Clinton Egbemhenghe (11)	44
Rebekkah Channer (7)	45
Austin Laylee (8)	45

St Agnes RC Primary School

Grace Robinson (10)	46
Sophie Clarke (8)	46
Amy McLaughlin (9)	47
Thomas Jones (9)	47
Anthony Dimaio (10)	48
Antonio Evangelista (8)	48
Daniel McCarthy (8)	49
Bernadette Sayers (9)	50
Lillo Eleftheriou (9)	50
Adam Monaghan (8)	51
Sian Murphy (10)	51
Daniel McCarthy (8)	52
Clare Allen (8)	52
Freddie Aleluya (7)	53
Emma Whelan (8)	53
Sean Keenan (7)	54
Ben Riddoch (8)	54
Natasha Kalule (6)	55
Sean Ekundayo (9)	55
Emily Cahill (10)	56

Anita Slowley (10)	56
Laura Tyther (10)	57
Joseph Badr (7)	57
Laura Riddoch (6)	58
Kathleen Street (10)	58
Gelsomina De Lucia (7)	59
Tom Hand (9)	59
George Osadebay (9)	60
Rebecca Whelan (6)	60
Hayley McCafferty (10)	60
Shane O'Gorman (6)	61
Siobhan Cloran (10)	61
Daniele Ignazi (9)	62
Jessica Nock (9)	62
Kofo Williams (6)	62
Monika D'Alessio (7)	63
Steven Linacre (5)	63
Daniella Ekundayo (7)	63
Kieran Abbott (7)	64
Bopski Mbadiwe (6)	64
Joseph White (7)	65
Megan Abbott (10)	65
Amaka Enenmoh (11)	66
Eleanor Smith (6)	66
Claire Gamble (11)	67
Daniela Massaro (6)	67
Tiffany Godfrey (7)	68
Callum Murray (5)	68
Roberto Evangelista (6)	68
Sebastian Tuck (6)	69
Adam Clark (6)	69
Ciara McAndrew (6)	69
Anthony Rogal (6)	70
Arthur Tyther (5)	70
Taylor Vigano (6)	70
Anthonia Bosah (5)	71
Aljan Idrissov (5)	71
Lily Korenhof (5)	71
Nana Esi Asabea Opoku-Adjei (11)	72
Jenny McCarthy (5)	72
Chris Nealon (11)	72
Jovelito R Suniga Jnr (6)	73

Christopher Osadebay (5)   73
James Gruy (6)   73
Brandon Roberts (7)   74
Nell Regan (5)   74
Clare Hand (11)   74
Jamie Harkin (11)   75
Eris Herbert (7)   75
Isabel Foulsham (10)   76
Bismark Bisquera (11)   76
Francie Smyth (11)   77
Claudine Kirby (11)   77
Katy McLaughlin (7)   78
Wyonna Loh (10)   78
Bridget Tighe (7)   79
Michael O'Connor (7)   79
Bruno Fernandes (7)   80
Alexander Craig (7)   80
Grace Kelly (7)   81
Hugo Lopez (7)   81

St Benedict's Junior School
Andrew Younger (8)   82
Daniel Gajkowski (9)   82
Tito Simonelli (9)   82
Harry McAdam (8)   83
Robert Picheta (9)   83
Aran Clifford (8)   84
Daniel Angwin (9)   84

St Gildas' RC Junior School
Joe Clift (8)   85
Caitriona Quinlan (9)   85
Monét Boyce-Nelson (9)   86
Esteban Lanao (8)   86
Taetum Lyons (9)   87
Shane Scott (8)   87
Andrew Dickson (10)   88
Timothy Peters (8)   88
Samantha Scott (10)   89
Tina Marfo Ruth (8)   89
Kitty Lees-Edmondson (10)   90

Connor Westbrook (9)	90
Tamara Prince-Gabb (10)	91
Nuala Reidy (8)	91
Elise McNamara (9)	92
Luke Scott (11)	92
Bonnie Benoiton (8)	93
Anthony Graham-Dillon (9)	93
Evelyn Gompertz (10)	94
Dalia Striganaviciute (8)	94
Shannah McGauran (8)	95
Kyle Joseph (9)	95
Anita Gmiat (11)	96
Shannon Bono (8)	96
Elizabeth Demetriou (10)	97
Rhianne Burnett (9)	97
Rowena Bicknell (11)	98
Lamar Esty (9)	98
Taylor Kershaw (11)	99
Jagoda Lisiecka (10)	99
Konnell Vassell (10)	100
Wendy Shoniregun (11)	101
Shauna Davis	102
Conor O'Leary (9)	102
Louise Millar (10)	103
Temitope Smith-Quim (10)	103
Dominic Canokema Kuluba (11)	104
Marcus Amaral Arrais (10)	104
Catalina Ogilvie-Browne (9)	105
Kadisha Knight (9)	105
Keith Adjei Twum Donker (10)	105
Rebecca Wilson (11)	106
Alexandra O'Keeffe (9)	106
Aisling Quinlan (11)	107
Niamh Byrne-Roberts (9)	107
Sean Crean (12)	108
Dillon Cuffe (9)	108
Marcos Fernandez (10)	109
Kathleen Carroll (9)	109
Roseanna Dundas (11)	110
Jim Walker (9)	110
Krystal Ude (8)	111
Samuel Fernandez (8)	111

Louis Hennessey-Hicks (10)	112
Mia Wolsey (8)	112
Isobel Sinnott (9)	113
Laurie Fitzgerald (8)	113
Liam Bligh (10)	114
Jessica Corrigan (8)	114
Tyrone Gaskin (10)	115
Danielle Sewell (9)	115
Holly Taylor (10)	116
Hayley Kimber (9)	116
Daniel Sexton (9)	117
Milena Messner (10)	117
Hope Merritt (10)	118
Kevin Donkor (10)	118
Aysha Starkey (9)	119
Mariella Lambrou (10)	119
Henry Garcin (11)	119
Clare Walton (10)	120
Reiss Taylor (9)	120
Victor Lopez (10)	121
Shannon Greenaway (10)	122
Jazz Lyons-Foster (11)	123
Katerina Makri (10)	124
Hannah Adelowo (11)	125
Joshua Morrison (10)	126
Magita Baidoo (10)	127

St Martin of Porres RC Primary School

Francesca Moglia (11)	128
Katie Foley (11)	128
Johann Rajakarunanayake (11)	129
Winston Osei Tu-Tu (10)	129
Laura Piccirillo (10)	130
Lauren Malone (11)	130
Erin Farrell (10)	131
Amira Gharbi (11)	131
Luke Mead (10)	132
Hannah McKirdy (10)	132
Alessandro Fontanini (11)	133
Elle Rolph (10)	133
Louise Parsons (10)	134

Ania Shannon (11)	135
Anya Fitzpatrick (10)	136

St Martin's Prep School
Simi Solebo (9)	136
Alexander Glassman (9)	136
Zachariah Johnson (9)	137
Brodie Berman (9)	137
Louie King (8)	138
Kayla Marks (10)	138
Erin-Louise Adams (8)	139
Sina Sharifi (10)	139
Ria Chitroda & Amber Patel (9)	140

Weston Park Primary School
Tom Andrews (10)	140
Shanti Chahal (9)	141
Ayla Richardson (11)	141
Dhru Patel (8)	142
Nina Rose Law Keen (7)	142
Lily Biglari (8)	143
Gwithyen Strongman (11)	143
Madeleine Sellers (7)	144
Owen Gillespie (7)	144
Louis Abbott Wilson (9)	145
Shyanne Duffus (8)	145
Lily Bradley (10)	146
Lucinda Hetherington (10)	147
Kairan Howard-Shawbell (9)	148
André Caudebec (9)	148
Boo Jackson (9)	149
Luke Rowan (10)	149
Sorcha Bradley (10)	150
Evie Lewis (9)	150
Karl Packham (9)	151
Emma Jimdar (8)	151
Scott Cadman (9)	152
Aisling Reidy Martin (9)	152
Megan Jones (9)	153
Eleni Odyssea Barnett (8)	153
Callum Midson	154

Laura Mokhtari (7)	154
Ellie Whitlock (7)	155
Joanna Clarke (8)	155
Joe Moody (9)	156
Jack Tully (9)	156
Elizabeth Norton (8)	157
Jian Chiang Poh (9)	157
Adrienne Webster (8)	158
Saffron Lashley (10)	158
Rufus Crewe-Henry (8)	159
Millie Page (8)	159
Ellen Gillespie (9)	160
Romany Crewe-Henry (11)	161
Jamilla Walcott (9)	162
Kamilah Jogee (7)	162
Helin Sertkaya (9)	163
Zulaikha Bedwei-Majdoub (10)	163
Deniz Genc (8)	164
Daisy Webb (9)	164
Jay-Ann Harriott (8)	165
Stephanie Saunders (8)	165
Bianca Kessna-Irish (11)	166

Wyvil Primary School

David Costa (10)	166
Rebekah Foster (9)	166
Zakwan Awangkechik (10)	167
Ti yanne Pemberton-Wright (8)	167
Sasha Ferdinand (9)	168
Jaylee Ali (10)	168
Abigail Ashmead (8)	169
Sarah Osei-Owusu (10)	169
Matilda Gunnery (9)	170
Alice Vilanculo (10)	170
Sammy Jo Handley (8)	171
Natasha Oviri (9)	171
Sara Andrade (10)	172
Daniel Ferreira (8)	173
Jermaine Elor (8)	173
Kennedy Mwangi (10)	174
Precious Ogbonna (10)	174

Jordan James (10)	174
Tyron Oyemade (9)	175
Ejiro Akpoveta (10)	175
Ishmael Daley (9)	175
Fatou Jobe (11)	176
Daniel Hurd (9)	176
Liliana Duarte (10)	177
Fabio Rodrigues (8)	177
Sophia Thompson (9)	178
Luis Gaudencio (8)	178
Jodeci Rowe-Matthews (11)	179
Hayden Morrison (8)	179
Raheema Abdirizaq (8)	180
Rasak Obanigba (9)	180
Asia Vassel (8)	180
Ibilola Macaulay (10)	181
Marcio Pereira (8)	181
Gustavo Honorato (9)	182
Elisabete Fernandes (9)	182

The Poems

Teacher's Torture

I was in the lesson disturbing the class
In all I was thinking of is staring at the glass
I was determined not to listen as I'd risen from the board.

I was bored of the teacher talking as I stumbled through my sleep.
I didn't do any work so I said a word and got detention.
I was in detention angry as can be
I never had the power to stop my angry temper.

I got out of school but I had homework to finish
But I had to do the dishes.
I went to lesson the next day
The teacher gave me grief when I said to her
'I'm the king of the school now, Miss.'

The teacher insulted me as I consulted the head of the school.
She got the sack and I packed my bags
And flew on line to Las Vegas.

Jack Day (10)
Latymer All Saints Primary School

Colourful Flowers

The spring is on its way
Lovely flowers every day
Snowdrops, violets, primroses,
Bluebells give a lovely hue
Lovely scents upon the breeze
Sometimes make people sneeze.
The summer comes and colours abound
Beautiful flowers all around
How wonderful the garden looks
It's like a lovely picture book.

Charlotte Wilson (11)
Latymer All Saints Primary School

My Class

My teacher's kind, my teacher's cool
My teacher always shows up for school.
My class is caring, my class is daring
Although some people are rubbish when sharing.

My class is the best football team
But for some classes this is their dream
We like English, we like RE
But most of all we love TV.

My class is never ashamed,
6 Vermilion that's our name!
We all really like to help Miss out
But to some people you have to shout!

My class is brainy and very smart
We learn things quickly, often by heart.
The tests we have are sometimes tricky
But we all think we are clever dickey.

When it's time to go home it's 3.15
Some want their homework because they're really keen
We get our coats and head for the door
And wonder what tomorrow has in store.

Andre Malik (11)
Latymer All Saints Primary School

Rainy Days

The fence was roaring, the cars were irritating,
The thunder went mad and the rain was pouring.
Everyone was running even the people without umbrellas
Were running with newspapers over their heads.
The cars were beeping like fire alarms.
People were delayed and they were shouting as if a shark or
Something had bit them.
And there's me; sitting alone in quiet, just watching this
And asking myself a question, what type of day is this?

Isaac Verissimo (10)
Latymer All Saints Primary School

Heaven

Heaven must be bright
Beaming with light
You'd feel lighter than air
You'd float without a care.

Flapping your wings with delight
Pondering whether you are wrong or right
As you approach the gate
You wonder if it is too late.

As you wait to be accepted
You are thankful you're not rejected
You begin to get ready,
For an afterlife of plenty.

In a place where the streets are paved with gold
That's what the Bible tells and told
I hope when my time does come,
This special place will be my home.

Tolu Olufemi (11)
Latymer All Saints Primary School

I Wish I Was An Eagle

I wish I was an eagle
So that I could fly through that open door.

I wish I was an eagle
So that I could soar my first soar.

I wish I was an eagle
So that I could touch the sky
And feel the tender clouds.

And at the end of the day
I could watch the sun touch the sea.

Lawrence Ife (10)
Latymer All Saints Primary School

I Wanna Be

I wanna be a clownfish
I will show off my rainbow colours
And will be popular also unique in the sea
Children will come with laughter and respect
After I will show them the magic of a clownfish.

Actually I'll be a teacher, my teacher Mrs Schuhmacher
As brave as a warrior fighting alone
Or maybe as bright as a pansy flower
However people will praise me like I am some sort of goddess
Then my tardiness will fly out and send my friendship to all.

I wanna be civil more as the Platinum
Surely I will get a music or sports career
Also follow my dream as a famous celebrity
I'll show you like, life that will always be mine
And you will surely see it all, all come true.

I wanna be tender, a hero or more
I'll spread butterflies or even TLC
My generation myself or maybe my kind
Will spread in my heart and bind with my soul
Have you ever seen pigs that fly?
Because maybe it surely will come by.

Priscilla Boateng (10)
Latymer All Saints Primary School

Dinosaurs

Centuries ago dinosaurs roamed the land,
The awesome carnivores had teeth as sharp as a gladiator's sword,
They walked through forests,
Eating and ripping flesh out of unprotected dinosaurs
With a 'crunch'.

Dinosaurs could smell fear and touch with their clawed feet
Taste the flesh of unprotected dinosaurs or the bitterness
Of the leaves high in the sky.

Charlie Cook (10)
Latymer All Saints Primary School

Hot Summer's Day

Hot summer's day
Children come out to play
Boring day for some
'Inside,' says their mum.

Soon when night falls
Girls put away their dolls
Tomorrow's another day
When the children come out to play.

They play in the sand
Pretend to be a band
Then there's a disaster
There comes the headmaster.

It is a school day
The children still play
They aren't ill
They just want to chill.

They should be in school
Instead of in the pool.

Stephanie Christos (10)
Latymer All Saints Primary School

The Lion's Den

Into the mouth of the lion's den
Crunch go the bones of an old dead hen
The roar as the lion sees me
He was going to eat me for his tea.

Claws raised, voice enhanced
He was going to get me, I had no chance
I don't know why you want to eat me
I haven't got a clue
I don't want to eat you
I just want to be friends with you.

Corrine Brown (11)
Latymer All Saints Primary School

Parents, Brothers And Sisters

Parents are so embarrassing
They go 'Are you alright darling?'
In front of all my friends
Couldn't my parents be a little less embarrassing?

Sisters are so annoying
They always want to know everything about me
My stuff gets really messed up
Why can't my sister be a little less annoying?

Brothers are such a pain
They take long in the bathroom but still smell
They always bring their girlfriends home
Why can't they be like angels?

My family is so boring
All they do is mope about
They never go to adventure parks
But instead they watch silly soaps.

Why can't my family be exciting?

Sheniqua Angus (11)
Latymer All Saints Primary School

Be Independent

When Beyoncé says, 'Me, Myself And I', I know what she means.
When J-Lo says, 'Love Don't Cost A Thing', I know what she means.
When Destiny's Child say, 'Independent Woman', I know what they mean.
When a woman says to a man, 'I hate you,' he is a coward to hit a woman.
Bob Marley says 'No Woman, No Cry'. They're not to cry.
Women of the world you've got it all
Boys can't spoil it.
Independent means survivor, on their own make it in the world
Not in need of a man.

Oluwaseun-Mae Adeneye (10)
Latymer All Saints Primary School

When I Wake Up In The Morning

When I wake up in the morning
I hear my birds singing in the garden
I hear my Mum say, 'Wake up it's time for school.'

When I wake up in the morning
I see the sun rise.
I see familiar faces of friends and family.

When I wake up in the morning,
I touch a nice cup of tea
That my mum brought to me.

When I wake up in the morning
I taste the taste of clean air.

When I wake up in the morning
I smell my breakfast in the oven
Cooking waiting for me.

Alice Suker (11)
Latymer All Saints Primary School

Future Changes

Look into the face
And see the trace of time
Look what it's done
Look at each line.

Spot the days of sunshine
In its history
Building destiny
In this ever changing world.

Vain hypocrites they challenge
This can't be denied
Demands thought for action
For reasons hold the key
To reveal the promise of a dream.

Malachi Dubarry (11)
Latymer All Saints Primary School

Perfume

If I was going to make perfume
I would add some flowers
Because they remind me of the smell.
If I was going to make perfume
I would add some lemon
Because it reminds me of the sun.
If I was going to make perfume
I would add some bananas
Because they remind me of the moon.
If I was going to make perfume
I would add some cherries
Because they remind me of a red rose.
I would add some chocolate
Because it reminds me of coffee.
I would add grass
Because it reminds me of the park.

Roqeeb Ajibola (8)
Loughborough Primary School

Perfume

If I was going to make perfume
I would add some cherries
They remind me of the rose.
I would add some blueberries
Because they remind me of the sea.
I would add some yellow pineapple
It reminds me of the sun.
I would add some mango
It reminds me of Jamaica.

Keani Kerr (7)
Loughborough Primary School

On The Tip Of My Tongue

I like fat fish.
I like chewy chicken.
I adore pepper and pizza.
I hate curly cabbage.
I can't stand black broccoli.
I really dislike soggy soup.
I hate green grapes.
I really dislike burnt buns.
I can't stand licking lollies.
I can't stand crunchy chips.
I really dislike slivery salami.
I hate licking liver.
I can't stand a-chewing apples.

Michaela Bowley (8)
Loughborough Primary School

Perfume

If I was going to make perfume
I would add some air freshener,
It reminds me of the sky.
I would put in some daffodils
They remind me of spring.
I would put in some nectar
It reminds me of bees.
I would put in some lavender
It reminds me of cups.
I would put in some caramel
It reminds me of the sun.
I would mix in some blackbirds
They remind me of blackberry pie.

Dean Robinson (7)
Loughborough Primary School

Perfume

If I was going to make perfume
I would add some cherries
They remind me of love.
Next I will put in violets
They remind me of the sea.
Then I would add green grass
It reminds me of the park.
And I will put in some pineapples
They remind me of the sun.
I will mix some toffee in
It will remind me of when I was in Margate
Playing in the sand.
I would like to add some oranges
They remind me of goldfish.

Morolayo Olatunde (8)
Loughborough Primary School

Perfume

If I was going to make perfume
I would put in some lemon
Because it reminds me of the sun.
If I was making perfume
I would add some sunflower
Because it reminds me of a hot summer's day.
If I was going to make perfume
I would stir in some apple
It reminds me of apple pie.
I would put in an orange
It reminds me of orange juice.
If I was going to make perfume
I would put in some sugarcane
It reminds me of the day I went to Jamaica.

Rashorn Evans (8)
Loughborough Primary School

My Secret Journey

I'm going on a secret journey
It's gonna be a surprise for you!
I'm gonna bring some food
As well as that I'll bring my older cousin Sue.
We're speeding down the road,
I see people and a lot of trash cans,
People coming in and out of shops.
A mother and daughter holding hands.
We were in a car and now we jump out.
We're right in front of Legoland.
Here's another surprise for you,
It's shut, what can we do?
We're going back home, we pass a shop,
What should we do? I think we should stop.
I'm standing outside the shop looking in the window.
Guess what I see? A box of Lego.
I'm gonna buy it and go back home,
I'm gonna build a funfair with it for my pet rat Poe.

Leah Williams (10)
Loughborough Primary School

My Wish

When I grow up I want to be a singer
They may ask me have I started?
I will say I'm just a beginner,
And on the way I will see lots of exciting things
And when I go on Top of the Pops, I'll wear lots of diamond rings.
They may cheer in my ear.
That's what I want!
I want to be a singer.
I hope my mum is proud of me!

Leann Byrne (9)
Loughborough Primary School

Guess Where I Am?

I come out the door,
I walk up the street,
I see some trees,
They are so beautiful,
They are green as grass,
And lovely coloured cars in front of me.
I see a tall building as I pass through,
I see a playground,
There are children playing and laughing,
And that's where I am going.
I hear a bell ringing,
Guess where I am?

Farhia Elmi (9)
Loughborough Primary School

The Road

I see a road
The dusty road.
A dusty road.
A man is singing.
A cat is jumping.
I see a road.
A dusty road.
A man is singing.
A cat is jumping.
A dog is barking.
I see a road.
A dusty road.
A man is singing.
A cat is jumping.
Do you know where I am?

Zam Zam Aden (9)
Loughborough Primary School

Journey On The Train

I see the grass as green as ever,
I see the car as fast as ever,
I see the boat sinking into the deep, deep water.

I see the tractor ploughing the field.
I see the houses going past me,
I see the school where children are learning
And I see me!

I see the park where children are playing.
I see the offices where adults are working.
I see a match where a man just scored.
Is that Michael Owen?

I see a shop where people are buying.
I see a pavement where teenagers are spitting.
I see a person giving money to the poor.
I see Mum unlocking the door.
I see Mum washing the floor.
I see Mum cooking food.
Oh no! I've missed my stop!

Abdirahim Ali (10)
Loughborough Primary School

My Dream

My dream is to have peace
My dream is to have lots of fun
My dream is to have lots of friends
My dream is to read good stories
My dream is to be funny
My dream is that sick people should get better
My dream is to help people
That's my dream.

Ruqayya Smith (10)
Loughborough Primary School

Love Hurts Badly

Where's my love gone?
I feel let down and crushed because I'm alone
In my dark, gloomy house.
I feel like I'm lost in my own dream world.
Fire goes through my soul and comes back out
Burning my soul.
I go speechless when my heart is broken.
I feel stressed when I'm hurt and start to pull out my hair.
I felt shocked when my boyfriend left me for someone else.
I feel like I've been removed from my sweet love.
Tears fall slowly from my watering eyes.
I feel dreadful and sad that my boyfriend chose that
beautiful Nina over me.
When I get pains in my stomach, I feel sad and lonely.
I remember the good times I had with him
And all the memories and pictures of me and him
And now they're gone forever and are never coming back.
What am I going to do?
I feel misunderstood,
I can't get him off my mind
He's gone and I can't get him back.

Rochelle Fraser (10)
Loughborough Primary School

A Journey To India

April the 10th today it is
Calendar's got a tick, better check quick.
In the car we are,
Dad's beeping, Mum's boring, brothers snoring!
Next thing I know I am asleep,
Waking up at Bombay.
Then changing at Bangalore.
Bangalore meet Mum's uncle Yash!
Getting in the Mercedes-Benz.

Khadijah Conroy (9)
Loughborough Primary School

The Mystical Rainforest

All the snowy, dark mountains high as the clouds.
The calm, cold rivers flow as soft as the blue sky.
Some brown and green leaves are as soft as feathers.
The small, blue flowers have great power.
The gigantic green trees are as green as grass.
The wooden branches are as hard as a table.
The hills are looking at me like eyes from far above.
All the brown trees' twigs look like a wig.

Ajibola Amire (9)
Loughborough Primary School

Beach Life

Colourful kites flying like silent birds.
Noisy people chatting like screeching parrots.
Hot sand burning like a sizzling fire.
Water flowing like a drifting cloud.

David O'Brien (10)
Loughborough Primary School

The Beautiful Girl

A beautiful girl's hair is like a waving tree
through the sky.
Her hair is as nice as a shining star.
Her hair is like a fire.
Her lips are light as the sun.
She is thinking about a holiday.
She looks like she needs a cup of tea by the fire.
Her pink lips shine in the mirror.
Her face is as dark as a black top.

Melika Williams (9)
Loughborough Primary School

Le Sechage Des Voiles

Blue sky sadly burning,
Calm sea flows away,
Little men walking fast,
Chubby women stuck badly,
Tall houses doing nothing happily,
Colourful walls still hot,
Stinky bin smelling badly,
Silver tap leaking heavily,
Big boats floating fast,
Fat trees waving roughly.

Nicole Voss (9)
Loughborough Primary School

The Beautiful Girl

Roses as red as blood
Flowers as beautiful as a flood
Dress as long as a tree
Hair as lovely as me
Earrings as shiny as gold
Eyes as blue as cold
Lips as bright as the sun
Nose as beautiful as my mum
Shirt as white as clouds
Hairband as wide as a crowd.

Ajibike Sobogun (9)
Loughborough Primary School

Sand Life

Colourful kites flying like quiet parrots.
Noisy people chatting like a loud factory.
Hot sand burning like an oven.
Broken down car stuck like hard ice.

Zachariah Ouazene (9)
Loughborough Primary School

Egyptian Statue

Egyptian hat and a gold face.
Ancient black eyes and colourful snakes.
King, ruler and a good god.
Shiny face and gold ears.
Green and gold Egyptian hat.
Good ruler and strong king.
Colourful colours and a gold body.

Jerlando Watson (9)
Loughborough Primary School

Feelings

I like the smell of strong flowers
Spreading across the land
And I sit down for hours trying to understand.
'Why are the hills covered with green grass Mum?'
'Because the rivers flood them up, right to the top
Then come back down again.'
The sky is brown and yellow mixed together,
And the trees are a browny green,
You see, I am very clever.

Sashkia Myers (10)
Loughborough Primary School

Tiger In A Tropical Storm

Tiger running as fast as can be
Wind blowing, you'll hardly ever see.
Lightning going at the speed of light,
Trees are having a fright.
Red flowers blowing, you'll see me in the night.
Tiger alone, away in the night.
Trees blowing through the light.

Daniel Kusimo (10)
Loughborough Primary School

The Egyptian Mask

Gold face and a shiny Egyptian hat.
Ancient black eyes and colourful snakes.
Small nose and red patterns.
A long chin and a kind Pharaoh.
Big lips and a good ruler.
A green god and an Egyptian face.

Nabiel Hafez (9)
Loughborough Primary School

A Wonderful Girl

A beautiful girl,
her hair is all in curls,
her lips shine like pearls,
she's all sad and lost,
all she can think about is,
he loves me, he loves me not.
Her hair is so powerful, like colourful fire,
her lips are waiting to kiss someone,
her curly hair is blowing in the blue sky,
she is thinking that she is going to meet
a kind gentleman.

Sharona Brown (9)
Loughborough Primary School

Strong Powerful Knights

Strong knights going into battle with powerful armour.
People killing at night-time in Britain.
Strong, rusted helmets on the cold floor.
Sharp, powerful spears gliding through the colourful sky.
The dark sky moving slowly and calmly like the blue water.
Tall flags moving in the dark, blowing, colourful sky.

Owen Barrett (10)
Loughborough Primary School

An Autumn Poem

Hard black conkers,
Crusty, red, brown leaves drop.
Hard black conkers,
Blank shiny conkers . . . fall.
Hard black conkers,
Furry squirrels run around.
Hard black conkers,
Silly robins sit on rusty trees.
Hard black conkers.

Ben McCormack (9)
Loughborough Primary School

Spiders

Spiders are happy and tickly.
Spiders like eating flies,
Spiders like to sleep on webs and flowers.
Spiders make me want to play football with them,
Spiders make me want to race them,
And I always win!

Kane Nosworthy (8)
Loughborough Primary School

Autumn Poem

Solid, hard, knobbly trees,
Bare and bony branches.
Solid, hard, knobbly trees,
Surrounded by invisible, cold and frosty air.
Solid, hard, knobbly trees,
Scampering, cheeky, furry squirrels.
Solid, hard, knobbly trees,
Animals get ready for winter hibernation.
Solid, hard, knobbly trees,
Leaves floating down like tiny feathers.

Rachel Ogunkoya (9)
Loughborough Primary School

Winter

Winter is very cold.
The squirrels are mad.
They think they're all bad.
Leaves fall off trees.
The birds are crazy.
The moles are lazy.
The leaves are red.
In winter you want to go to bed.

Imran Hussain (9)
Loughborough Primary School

An Autumn Poem

Crispy, crunchy, rusty red leaves,
Through lots of branches, falling.
Crispy, crunchy, rusty red leaves,
Falling on pretty squirrels.
Crispy, crunchy, rusty red leaves,
The lovely trees are breaking down.
Crispy, crunchy, rusty red leaves,
The death cloak of leaves is falling.
Crispy, crunchy, rusty red leaves,
Spring - the end of death.

Desré Denton-Ashley (8)
Loughborough Primary School

The Waves

The sea will rise slowly
The forces of wind shall make it cry
It will get stronger as it cries
Lightning struck by day and night
It will calm down as the sun shines
Peace at last.

Deborah Adelabu (9)
Loughborough Primary School

The Last Night

It's not a starry night
It has no light
It's not bright!
It's dark, you hear dogs bark
With a loud *woof!*
Trees look like monsters
A boy walked with scary motion
The monster's hairy limbs are reaching . . .
You should beware.

Natalie Robertson (9)
Loughborough Primary School

My Wonder!

I wonder why I live
I wonder why I wonder
I asked my mum
I asked my dad
They said, 'Your wonders are beautiful.'
I wondered, was it true?
It could be a lie.
My wonders!

Francisco Norena-Gallego (10)
Loughborough Primary School

An Autumn Poem

Crispy, crunchy, rusty red leaves,
Dropping from the narrow trees.
Crispy, crunchy, rusty red leaves,
Black conkers falling from the tree.
Crispy, crunchy, rusty red leaves,
Squirrels scamper up the naked tree.
Crispy, crunchy, rusty red leaves,
Crumbled leaves floating from the willow trees.

Danielle Crawford-Gartell (9)
Loughborough Primary School

It Is All About Me

My name is Mariam,
It is all about me.
I like to eat fish,
It is all about me.
I like to play with my sisters,
It is all about me.
I like to paint,
It is all about me.
I like to come to school,
It is all about me.
I like to have fun with my friends,
It is all about me.
I like to read poems which are all . . .
About me!

Mariam Elmi (9)
Loughborough Primary School

Autumn Leaves

Crispy, crunchy, yellow leaves,
Birds singing every day, singing nice autumn songs.
Crispy, crunchy, yellow leaves,
Hard leaves, horribly cold.
Crispy, crunchy, yellow leaves,
Snails are moving so slow people get angry.
Crispy, crunchy, yellow leaves,
Bony, bare, lumpy trees hard as can be.
Crispy, crunchy, yellow leaves,
Yellow, red and green trees.

Isabel Ribeiro (9)
Loughborough Primary School

Children Talking, Children In The Hall

Children talking
Children in the hall
Teachers shouting
Everyone is well
Children playing ball
The playground bell has rung
Teachers are getting ready for work
People are eating buns
Everyone is having fun.

Jason Appeagyei-Boachie (9)
Loughborough Primary School

A Journey To Different Planets

I went to Mars,
and I bought some chocolate bars.
I went to Jupiter,
and I saw a superstar.
I went to Saturn,
and I bought a red button.
I went to Venus,
and I measured in metres.
I went to the sun,
and I bought a red bun,
and it was all really, really fun.

Ebtihal Saleh (9)
Loughborough Primary School

An Autumn Poem

Naughty green robin,
Rusty, brown leaves drop.
Naughty green robin,
Sitting on a rough, scrappy, hard branch.
Naughty green robin,
Crunching, mashing conkers.
Naughty green robin,
Playing with naughty brown squirrels.
Naughty green robin.

Azharul Islam
Loughborough Primary School

A Scary Night

It was a scary night
When the hills were dark
Water was falling
Falling too calm and too still.
Owls were hooting, wings were flapping,
It was a scary night
Too scary to be in the dark.

Merve Etem (8)
Loughborough Primary School

Happy Valentine

To my true love,
Valentine's Day is a time to say it's true,
I really do love you, because you have lots of love.
You sing like a dove,
You have lots of warmth in your heart,
You have lovely art,
I would like to dance the night away,
But I really can't stay.
From your Valentine.

Regina Okeke (9)
Loughborough Primary School

An Autumn Poem

Bare, bony, brown tree,
Looks like a person's knee.
Bare, bony, brown tree
Black conkers on the floor.
Bare, bony, brown tree,
Rusty red leaves surround the tree like
a skirt.
Bare, bony, brown tree,
Rusty brown squirrels climbing up the tree.
Bare, bony, brown tree.

Jadian Effik (8)
Loughborough Primary School

This Is My Life

This is my life that used to be different,
I am the girl that used to be innocent.

I am sad, my face is down,
I'm not that usual happy clown.

What happened to the love and sunshine?
I didn't know my life would just be mine.

I'm on my own, standing up,
I used to be a happy pup.

Why is my life going wrong?
Isn't it supposed to be quite long?

Why is my life starting to change?
Why is it going terribly strange?

It feels like my life is floating away,
After that I won't see another day.

Ophelia Gibson Best (10)
Reay Primary School

Pollution

We drop litter on the street,
People leave rubbish at our feet,
Cars drive around with all their fumes,
From all the cars a black cloud looms.

Beer can holders that need to be cut,
Who threw down that cigarette butt?
Nobody, nobody, nobody knows,
How long that will take to decompose.
All I see is abandoned cans,
I look on the road, so many vans.

We drop litter on the street,
People leave rubbish at our feet,
Cars drive around with all their fumes,
From all the cars a black cloud looms.

I look to my left and see flats with graffiti,
I look to my right and see a wrapper from a sweetie.
People decided to recycle in a factory,
People decided it's better actually,
I see billowing smoke,
Enough to make you choke.

We drop litter on the street,
People leave rubbish at our feet,
Cars drive around with all their fumes,
From all the cars a killer cloud looms.

Hester Carter (10)
Reay Primary School

The Sandwiches

Ella made some sandwiches on a sunny day,
Ella made some sandwiches in the month of May.
Ella made some sandwiches with lots of rusty nails,
A worm and a snake and lots of powdered snails.
She kicked it, she slapped it, she hit it with her head,
She slapped it, she whacked it and slept with it in bed.

Luke Wallace-Worrell (7)
Reay Primary School

Why?

Why are we called humans?
Why is silk so silky soft?
Why can't we fly like birds?
Why is life so dangerous?

Why, why, why, why?
Why are shops called shops?
Why is the Queen called a queen?
Why can't I climb a building?
Why can't we just be ourselves?

Why do people murder?
Why do people sing?
Why do people dance so much?
Why are people allergic to stuff?

Why, why, why, why?
Why are shops called shops?
Why is the Queen called a queen?
Why can't I climb a building?
Why can't we just be ourselves?

Why is the world not flat?
Why are dogs in the pound?
Why are dodos extinct?
But most of all,
Am I asking why, too much, you think?

Clara Hallifax (11)
Reay Primary School

The Pancake

The teacher made a pancake with spiders,
apple stew and a dog.
The teacher made a pancake with lots of hairy logs.
The teacher made up a cake and gave it to the kids.
It killed them slowly and they turned into pigs . . .
    And I'm the teacher.

Sarah Agui (7)
Reay Primary School

Sweet Sunset Beach

There's a sunset on the beach today
The wind
Is as warm as a mother who cradles her baby
The clouds
Look like candyfloss from the fair
Red, orange, pink and purple
The sea is like a tear
Warm and salty
The sand is like sawdust
Crunching under my feet
The boats in the sea are floating around
Like birds in the sky
The people playing
Are like kittens and a ball of yarn
As I walk away
The beach is engulfed in darkness
Like someone's put out a candle.

Lauren Burrows (10)
Reay Primary School

Marvellous Magical Bread

The baker baked some magic bread
in the month of May.
The baker baked some magic bread
On his 21st birthday.
The baker baked some magic bread
He filled it with bugs and worms, creepy-crawlies
And an ant which really made it squirm.

He mashed it, he squashed it, he slapped it on his head,
He kicked it, he whipped it, he slept with it in bed.

Alysha-Rae Weekes (8)
Reay Primary School

Holidays Are Fun

A holiday,
really does pay,
I will never,
forever
hate a holiday.
I love the sea,
the yellow sand,
the green land,
pick the shells,
hear the bells,
I feel really cool,
when I'm swimming in the pool.
I adore the tasty food,
I'm always in a happy mood.
dogs bark,
in the park,
fly to the moon
in June
holidays are fun.

Karim Boustani (9)
Reay Primary School

The Disgusting Pancake

The baker made some pancakes with mice and dice and head lice.
The baker made some pancakes with lots of chomping dogs,
The baker made some pancakes,
He gave them to the king,
They made him sick for fifty years
And turned him right red and green.

He mushed it, he crushed it, he threw it on the floor,
He kissed it, he hugged it, he brushed it on the wall.

George Hodgkinson (7)
Reay Primary School

Big Cats

Big cats living everywhere
Leopards using trees as chairs
Lions prowling round at night
Hunting 'til the morning light
Tiger with its stripy tail
Slowly hearing it wail for

Freedom.

Zoos locking them in cages
People staring at them for ages
Them pacing up and down
Searching for the crown
They had back then.

So please give them
Freedom.

Happy times 'cause spring has come
Baby cubs, their walking begun
They are in a happy place
Where no one hunts the big cat race.

Those cubs were lucky
'cause they have

Freedom.

Georgia Whitaker-Hughes (10)
Reay Primary School

The Teacher Made Some Syrup

The teacher made some syrup on a Saturday.
The teacher made some syrup in the month of May.
The teacher made some syrup, she filled it with hot chocolate,
A spider, a tiger and a clumsy biker.
She kicked it, she licked it, she threw it on the floor,
She chomped it, she stomped on it and it slithered out the door.

Constance Egbemhenghe (8)
Reay Primary School

Happiness

Go on to the football pitch
You will see a flying witch
She will shout out, 'Ashley Cole
Scored a goal.'

If you see a snail
Don't go all pale
Have a little smile
Make it worth your while.

If you see a bumblebee
It will lead you to a tree
A ring on a boat
With a brightly coloured coat.

Teachers at school
Are not all cool
Some sit on stools
And act like fools.

Be silent
Don't be violent
When you go to bed and snore
Don't forget to close the door.

Esavon Petersen (10)
Reay Primary School

The Farmer Made A Biscuit

The farmer made a biscuit on a windy day,
He did it so he could waste the time away.
He put in lots of jelly,
As he watched his boring telly.
The farmer made a biscuit, on a windy day.
He mushed it, he crushed it,
He sometimes just brushed it!

Lily Paine (8)
Reay Primary School

Don't Waste Paper!

All day in schools we're wasting paper,
all day in offices we're wasting paper.

But if anyone would stop and think,
about all the animals with nothing to drink,
what a difference it would make,
what a difference.

All you have to do is reuse paper,
don't just throw it in the bin,
what a sin,
what a sin,
would you like to be killed or left with no home?
Just because of mean humans,
cutting down our trees?
Who saw down the homes of bumblebees,
no, I didn't think so,
I didn't think so.

Just remember these words,
reuse, recycle, reduce,
and keep them in your heart,
then at least we can make a start,
on saving our animals,
and telling people the paper rules.

If we can keep them,
we've made a start,
at saving our world and the animals at its heart.
Help save our world and animals!

Alice Hirst (10)
Reay Primary School

I Believe

I believe
That there is world peace
On this planet
We live on.

I believe
Racism can stop
That we can fight it
Every race is important
And that should stand for everyone.

I believe
That guns should not sell
That violence can stop
And this world can be a better place
And we can keep it a better place.

If I did not believe
I would forget about
World peace.

I know every day, someone dies,
I believe we can stop this
Just believe.

So I believe there is hope
And I hope
That when there's violence and hunger
We can stop it
That's what I believe.

Dean Bright (11)
Reay Primary School

Science

Thanks for the science that makes me write
Thanks for the science that makes me bright
Thanks for the science that makes the light
Thanks for the science that makes our sight
Thanks for the science that's so exciting
Look at me now, I love writing.

Thanks for the science that helps us move
And thanks for the science that makes us groove
Thanks for the science that makes us sure,
Thanks for the science, if not, no cure,
Thanks for the science that makes things bubble
Thanks for the science that made the telescope hubble.

Now we've had a look at science
We all know *science needs more clients!*

Erick Hinds (10)
Reay Primary School

Football

He kicks the ball into the net,
Everyone has won their bet,
People weren't being very fair
It has turned into a great nightmare.

Oh no, it's a foul,
The crowd gave a howl,
They've thrown in a towel,
To mop up the blood,
Mixed with mud,
Because of a stud.

He's been carried away,
To a hospital bay,
Where he painfully lay,
Until another day.

Miles Millward (11)
Reay Primary School

My Uncle Tony

His hair is as sharp as a lethal dagger,
When I see him I begin to stagger
His walking stick is as long as a giraffe's neck,
When I see him I think, *what the heck!*
His feet are manky
His arms are lanky
His legs are bony
He is moany
His feet are smelly
He's got a fat belly
He likes to go swimming
With lots of old women
His teeth are as yellow as the sun
When I'm with him it's not much fun
But when I'm not I'm proud and free,
I've escaped his nails that sting like a bee
Well that's the story of my uncle Tony,
By the way his favourite food is mushed up
    Balony!
    Yuck!

Jon Dartnell (9)
Reay Primary School

Ten Things Found In A Footballer's Pocket

A little teddy mascot saying 'I love you'.
A smelly pair of blue socks.
A crinkled green support bandage.
A screwed up £50 note.
Zizzing stolen whistles from the ref.
A mobile phone with polyphonic ring tones.
Pens for autographs.
A pink sweat band.
A red card.
A muscle-boosting energy drink.

Jessica Kelly (10)
Reay Primary School

Homework

Homework is so boring
It makes you go off snoring
It wastes your free time
And makes children whine.

So if you don't like it
You should deny it
I think it's confusing
I'd rather be snoozing.

Why?
I could lie down and die
It makes you no better
It doesn't make you clever.

You could be doing football
But homework duty calls
Instead you are stuck inside
In a homework landslide.

So please teachers give us a break
There isn't much more we can take
So children listen to me
Then we can be finally free.

Sophie Hale (10)
Reay Primary School

Pancake

The cook made a pancake on the month of May
The cook made a pancake on a holiday
The cook made a pancake,
He filled it with rotten snakes
And egg and a child and lots and lots of rakes!

Beatrice Chamberlain-Kent (7)
Reay Primary School

The Teachers In Our School

The teachers in our school
I think they're really cool.

Miss Jean eats yellow peas
Mr Hogs has chickenpox
Mrs Flairs has blue hairs
Mr Brown always has a frown
Mrs Beckham always says, 'To heck with 'em'
Mr Fly likes expired pies
Miss Blue wears odd shoes
And this is the funniest of all

Mr Hays thinks he's tall
But is in fact very small.

Lola Meghoma (10)
Reay Primary School

Thank You Music

Thank you for the music beat
Thanks for the music in our feet
Thank you for the songs that rhyme
Thanks for the music that keeps time.

Thank you for the music that makes me dance
And some that put me in a trance
Thanks for music in a hall
Brightened up with a disco ball.

Thank you for music that makes me groove
And that which makes me really move
Thank you for the music with jive and jiggle
And that which makes me prance and wiggle.

Thanks for the music that we reach and touch
Thank you, very, very much.

Omari Okwulu (10)
Reay Primary School

Saturday Morning

Saturday morning you fall asleep
Saturday morning you need to eat
Saturday morning you have a shower
Saturday morning you think *whatever.*
Saturday morning you eat Coco Pops
Saturday morning you shout, 'How did I get the chickenpox?'
Saturday morning you watch TV
Saturday morning you see your friend Lee.
Saturday morning you feel a bit odd
Saturday morning you call a big mob
Saturday morning you think, *what if I get caught?*
Saturday morning you doze off
Saturday morning your parents shout, 'What?'
Saturday morning you say, 'Oh my God.'
    'It's Sunday morning, come on we're off.'

Sophia Nesro (11)
Reay Primary School

My Friend Fred

I have a friend called Fred
His body's like a bed
He has a nose
Just like a rose
He can jump as high as a happy frog
And can talk as loud as a barking dog.
As well as that,
His shoes are like canoes!
And he has a coat
That's made out of a goat!
He has a jumper that looks like a bumper
He wears a diaper because he is hyper!
    And he likes to eat meat!

Oscar Rainbird-Chill (8)
Reay Primary School

The Bus Driver Made A Cake

The bus driver made a cake on a Monday,
The bus driver made a cake on a warm day,
The bus driver made a cake, he filled it with hot dogs,
Then he added a fish or two
Then a snake in sauce.
He spilled it, he whacked it,
And made it very hot,
He baked it, he kicked it,
And did a little jog.

The bus driver made a cake with fish, figs and cogs,
The bus driver made a cake and filled it with lots of stomping frogs.
The bus driver made a cake
And gave it to his wife,
It made her sick for fifty years and . . .
ruined her life.

Joe Knight (8)
Reay Primary School

The Teacup Man

There's this teacup man
His name is Stan
He's very funny and very grand
He doesn't like houses
He lives in a van
Even though he has a caravan.
He's changed his name to Sam
And he is a Yorkshireman.
If you want to see him he will always be down
In Yorkshire with his brother in a van.

Joseph Duggan (7)
Reay Primary School

The Beach

At the beach it's fun
And there is lots of sun
It's really cool
And it's got a pool
It's got lots of sand
I get really, really tanned.

At the beach it's great
I play there with my mate
I look at the exotic fish
Sometimes they come as a dish
There's a beach near me
People there drink ice tea
Sometimes the waves get high
But I've got to say, bye-bye.

Nina Carter (8)
Reay Primary School

The Noise

It was late at night when I heard a noise
It was coming from my chest of toys
I sat up straight and looked around
On the ceiling on the ground
At the window by the door
Then I got my slippers that were on the floor
The noise was big, the noise was great
And straight away I rang a mate
I told her there was a really loud noise
Coming from my chest of toys
And she said, 'How does it sound,
This really loud noise?'
And I said, '*Bing, bang*
   Ting, tang
      Zoom!'

Taylor Loring (9)
Reay Primary School

Sailing

I love the way the anchor chain rattles
Pulling and heaving on its many shackles
I love the way we go so fast,
Even motorboats can't go past.

The water is foaming
People are beachcombing
The fish are swimming
The sun has started dimming.

The wind is blowing
The motor is slowing
The sun is setting
There's fish in the netting!

The captain is shouting
The whales are spouting
The sail is flapping
The water is lapping.

I just smile and smile
As we go mile after mile
I'm falling into a marvellous dream
Of going to watch a lifeboat team.

The flag is flying
The crew are sighing
The boat's name is 'Bright Selina'
But I like the name 'Zerina'.

The sea is rocking
I watch the wind stocking
This is boat life
It's good but full of strife!

Martha Dillon (8)
Reay Primary School

My Favourite Things

Sports cars and movies
And discos that are groovy
Hockey and football
And cool swimming pools
Burgers and chicken wings.

These are a few of my favourite things.

Racing with bikes,
And going on hikes,
Reading my book and
Helping Dad cook.
Going to cinemas
And playing snooker at bars,
Listening to how Michael Jackson sings.

These are a few of my favourite things.

Titan Fiennes Tiffin (8)
Reay Primary School

Pets

I want to buy a pet
I want to buy my mum a pet
But I can't decide which one to get
I want to get the funky monkey

Should I get that mouse in that house?
Or should I get that cat it will match with her hat?
Or should it be that pig that wears a wig?

Should I get that tiger it is quite a hider?
Or should I get that dog it looks quite like a hog?
Or that snake sliding around the rake?

I've got the hider, yes the tiger,
I hope she likes it, yes I do.

Kazden Farruggio (9)
Reay Primary School

The Ice Cream

The cat made some ice cream on a sunny day
The cat made some ice cream in the month of May.
The cat made some ice cream
She filled it with some slugs
A fish and a magpie, and loads of ugly worms.
She bashed it, she crashed it, she filled it with old socks,
She squished it, she squashed it, it made her eyeballs pop.

The cat made some ice cream with flies and pies and ties
The cat made some ice cream with lots of mean magpies
The cat made some ice cream and gave it to a dog
It made him green and very mean for 8000 years!
He bashed her, he thrashed her,
He hit her with a log,
He smashed her, he crashed her,
And made her eat a frog!

Ella Morphet (7)
Reay Primary School

The Beach

Here at the beach
There are tasty ice creams
There are joyful screams
Chips and fish
Is the best dish.

Here at the beach
Children playing high and low
We'll be here you know
Come to the beach today.

Ellen Cullen (8)
Reay Primary School

I Believe

I believe
That black and white are alike
They can mix and can live without racism in this world.

I believe
That life is too short
To be wasted on war
The world should be about freedom
. . . Happiness.

I believe,
There should be no such thing as
Poor and rich people
That everybody should get the
Same amount of money.

I believe
People should be treated the same
Disabled and wheelchair people
There should be more ramps on
Pavements and shops.

If I did not believe
I would stop writing
But I do believe so I've
Carried on writing.

I know that every year
80,000 people die of cancer
So I'm asking you please
To donate money for . . .
People in need.

I believe in you
So why not believe in me?

Clinton Egbemhenghe (11)
Reay Primary School

The Crumbly Coffee

The teacher made a coffee on her birthday,
The teacher makes her coffee in every single way,
The teacher made a coffee and filled it with syrup,
A blob of sugar and a drop of butter,
And a scoop of strawberry jam.
She mixed it, she whisked it, she gave it a great big whack,
She crushed it, she mushed it, she dropped it on the crack.

The teacher made a coffee with socks and rocks and blocks
The teacher made a coffee with lots of wriggling clocks
The teacher made a coffee and gave it to the head
It made him red and he slept in the shed until he found a bed.
He kicked her, he flicked her, he whacked her round the head.
He squashed her, he squished her, he hit her with some lead.

Rebekkah Channer (7)
Reay Primary School

The Baker

The baker made a sandwich on a boiling day
The baker made a sandwich, it was in the middle of the day
The baker made a sandwich he put in some sauce, a monkey,
a rat and lots and lots of chilli sauce.
He pushed it, he whacked it, he threw it on his back
He kicked it, he stepped on it, he threw it in his sack

The baker made a sandwich, he added an old clock
The baker made a sandwich, he added a banana
A flower, a flower pot and the Ramayama.
He kicked it, he pinched it, he threw it on the floor
He crushed it, he scrunched it, it flew out the door.

Austin Laylee (8)
Reay Primary School

New Clothes

Dear Diary
I got me some new dresses,
Some new dresses for me,
One with a bow and one with a bee,
One for the summer and one for the ball,
One for the party and one for the mall.

I got me some new skirts,
Some new skirts for me,
One for the christening, and one for the sea.
One for the disco and all for me.

I got me some new tops,
Some new tops for me,
One for dinner and one for tea,
One for the holiday, and one for the term,
One for the church, and one that says 'learn'.

Dear Diary, this cost a bomb,
So I ended up nicking the lot from my mum,
It was fun, it was great . . . see you soon.
    Love Grace.

Grace Robinson (10)
St Agnes RC Primary School

I Think Of You

When I see the sun I think of you
When I feel the rain it makes me blue
When I smell the snow I think of you
For my love for the world is honest and true.

When I feel the cold it brings me down
When I see you I laugh like a clown
When I smell the fresh green grass, I feel as good as new
For my love of the world is honest and true.

Sophie Clarke (8)
St Agnes RC Primary School

John And Jane

John likes green things
Things that grow
Long, tall grass.

Jane likes yellow
Things that are hot
Blazing sunshine.

John likes green things
Things that grow
Juicy green apples.

Jane likes yellow things
Things that are hot
Tasty custard.

Jane says, 'Butter.'
John says, 'Lime.'
Jane says, 'Yellow lines.'
John says, 'Slime.'

John says, 'Apples.'
Jane says, 'Mustard.'
John says, 'Leaves.'
Jane says, 'Custard.'

John and Jane will never agree
Until lemons and apples grow
On one tree.

Amy McLaughlin (9)
St Agnes RC Primary School

What Is The Snow?

It is a white blanket hiding the world
It is a spilt bottle of milk all over the floor
It is a piece of sparkling ice covering everything
It is a big white cloud fallen from the sky
It is sparkling glitter fallen from the clouds.

Thomas Jones (9)
St Agnes RC Primary School

My Cats

Archie, my black cat is big and bold
He never does, as he is told
He sleeps all day as he is out all night
What he gets up to would give me a fright.

He loves his food, which puts him in a good mood
His favourite is meat, especially lamb.
He does not like bacon, cheese or ham,
He gets very cross if you give him Spam.

Polly is his sister, who Archie thinks is a wally,
Polly likes to be next to a nice warm dolly.
Polly loves to have some fish,
So when she's finished she licks her dish.

I love both my cats as you can see
I would not sell them for 50p.
When I am at school I know they miss me
What a lucky boy I am, whoopee! Whoopee!

Anthony Dimaio (10)
St Agnes RC Primary School

Pet Poems

In his bedroom Antonio kept . . .

Ten goldfish swimming in water
Nine monkeys swinging on the light
Eight cats chasing the mice
Seven mice running away from the cats
Six snakes slithering on the floor
Five dogs sitting on the bed barking
Four mice squeaking very quietly
Three donkeys who lived under the bed
Two foxes making shadows
And one, guess what?

Antonio Evangelista (8)
St Agnes RC Primary School

Jane And John

John likes green things
Things that grow
Juicy green apples.

Jane likes yellow things
Things that are hot
Blazing sunshine.

John likes green things
Things that grow
Caterpillars and grass.

Jane likes yellow things
Things that are hot
Baby chicken and chips.

John likes green things
Things that grow
Lime and seaweed.

Jane likes yellow things
Things that are hot
Sweetcorn and sand.

Jane says, 'Butter.'
John says, 'Lime.'
Jane says, 'Yellow lines.'
John says, 'Slime.'

John says, 'Grass.'
Jane says, 'Custard.'
John says, 'Caterpillar.'
Jane says, 'Mustard.'

Jane and John will
Never agree till
Lemons and apples grow on the
Same tree.

Daniel McCarthy (8)
St Agnes RC Primary School

Never Agree

John likes green things
Things that grow.

Jane likes yellow things
Things that are hot.
Blazing sunshine.

John likes green things
Things that grow.
Juicy green apples.

Jane likes yellow things
Things that are hot.

Jane says, 'Custard.'
John says, 'Lime.'
Jane says, 'Mustard.'
John says, 'Slime.'
Jane says, 'Butter.'
John says, 'Apples.'
Jane says, 'Lemons.'
Jane and John will never agree
Until lemons and limes grow on the same tree.

Bernadette Sayers (9)
St Agnes RC Primary School

Peter's Pets

In his bedroom Peter kept . . .
Ten white cats in the wardrobe
Nine monkeys swinging on the light bulb
Eight black dogs on the window
Seven pink hamsters crawling around the room
Six rats walking fast
Five goldfish in a bowl swimming around
Four muddy pigs in the cupboard
Three earwigs that scuttled and hit
Two giraffes under Peter's bed
And one . . . guess what?

Lillo Eleftheriou (9)
St Agnes RC Primary School

John And Jane

John likes green things
Things that grow
Juicy green apples

Jane likes yellow things
Things that are hot
Blazing sunshine

John likes green things
Things that grow
Kiwi fruit.

Jane likes yellow things
Things that are hot
Chips and maggots.

Jane says, 'Butter.'
John says, 'Lime.'
Jane says, 'Yellow lines.'
John says, 'Lime.'

John says, 'Apples.'
Jane says, 'Mustard.'
John says, 'Leaves.'
Jane says, 'Custard.'

Jane and John will never agree till
Apples and bananas grow on one tree.

Adam Monaghan (8)
St Agnes RC Primary School

The Golden Eagle

The dominant predator who lives in mountainous places,
Gliding over mountains with its long wings and long broad tail.
The scavenging eagle soars through the sky,
Sharp eyes glaring from his golden head.
Silently swooping down and attacking its prey,
Its long talons dig into small birds and mammals,
Carrying it back to its eyrie to feed its hungry eaglets.

Sian Murphy (10)
St Agnes RC Primary School

Yellow Things, Green Things

John likes green things, things that grow, juicy, green apples.
Jane likes yellow things, things that are hot, blazing sunshine.
John likes green things, frogs in grass.
Jane likes yellow things, rubber ducks swimming.
John likes green things, slobby, blobby slime.
Jane likes yellow things, eating chips on the sand.
John likes green things, Kiwi fruit and seaweed.

Jane says, 'Butter.'
John says, 'Lime.'
Jane says, 'Yellow lines.'
John says, 'Slime.'
John says, 'Apples.'
Jane says, 'Mustard.'
John says, 'Leaves.'
Jane says, 'Custard.'

Daniel McCarthy (8)
St Agnes RC Primary School

A Celebration Poem

The invitation sent, the date and time announced
The wedding bells ring out.

The bride walked up the aisle in white, it was a lovely sight.
The groom looked around and gave a smile.

Then the priest read out the vows, the bride and groom replied,
'I do.'

The organ played the wedding march
The confetti fill the air
The photographer clicked away
A day to remember.

Clare Allen (8)
St Agnes RC Primary School

What Is Red?

Red is a ball
That boys and girls can play with.
Red is a rose
For your mum and dad.
Red is a valentine card.
Red is blood
That's in your body.
Red is a robin
That flies in the air.
Red is a dress
When you go to bingo.
Red is a pencil
To colour in a picture.
Red is a lipstick
For your mummy.

Where would we be without the colour red?

Freddie Aleluya (7)
St Agnes RC Primary School

Emma's Pets

I had a dog, the dog dug,
The dog dug deep into the earth.

I had a duck
The duck flew, the duck flew far.

I had a flea, the flea jumped,
The flea jumped high into the sky.

I had a snake and it kept me up
By hissing and hissing all night and day.

I had a monkey, the monkey swung
The monkey swung in the trees.

Emma Whelan (8)
St Agnes RC Primary School

What Is Red?

Red is a robin
that you see in the tree.
Red is lava
that comes from a volcano.
Red is a rose
that is prickly.
Red is a postbox
that you put letters in.
Red is an apple
crunchy and sweet.
Red is the sun
that is bright and blazing hot.
Red is a flag
that you wave about.
Red is a rocket
that goes up to the moon.

Where would we be without the colour red?

Sean Keenan (7)
St Agnes RC Primary School

Ben's Pets

In Ben's bedroom Ben kept . . .
Ten hamsters climbing in their cage
Nine fish splashing water in their tank
Eight dogs chasing cats
Seven fat pigs being lazy
Six cats running away from the dogs
Five snakes sliding on the ground
Four rats running around
Three blind mice
Two beetles making me scared
And one . . . guess what?

Ben Riddoch (8)
St Agnes RC Primary School

What Is Red?

Red is a toy car
that you get for Christmas.

Red is a lipstick
that mums put on their lips.

Red is a rose
that smells sweet and nice.

Red is an apple
that is juicy and scrummy.

Red is a heart
that you give to your mummy on Valentine's Day.

Red is a woolly jumper
that you wear when it's cold.

Red is tomato ketchup
that I like eating with chips.

Natasha Kalule (6)
St Agnes RC Primary School

Sean's Pets

In Sean's bedroom he kept . . .
Ten earwigs that scuttled and hid
Nine spiders that wove their webs
Eight white mice with pink little eyes
Seven hamsters that snoozed in the cage
Six black cats who were after the mice,
Five big dogs under the bed,
Four pigs, lazy and fat,
Three goldfish swam about all day,
Two lions roaring all night and day,
And one, guess what?

Sean Ekundayo (9)
St Agnes RC Primary School

Dogs

Dogs, dogs everywhere, up here, down there
You bark, you stare, looking anywhere.

Dogs, dogs, running and walking
You jog, you fetch, you play.

Dogs, dogs, playful creatures,
You all have good features.

Dogs, dogs, you play fetch
You play ball, run then stretch.

Dogs, dogs, you're so cute,
Sausage, bulldog and others.

Dogs, dogs, you're so clever
Dogs you are tricksters.

Dogs, dogs, eating and eating
You bark, jog, play and you love *bones!*

Emily Cahill (10)
St Agnes RC Primary School

My Pet

My pet is called Lucy
She is the wonderful age of five
She does not have any children
But she really likes to hide
She is a sweet, loving cat
And she really doesn't bite
But when it is extra dark
She has a really big fright.
She is a lovely cat with a spot on each side
But the thing she likes to do most is have her own pride.

Anita Slowley (10)
St Agnes RC Primary School

The Dog Called Rover

There was once a dog called Rover,
Who was very active and always tumbling over
He loved to play with balls especially with the children,
The children used to always call, 'Rover, Rover, Rover!'

Rover was a lovely dog and everyone liked him,
Rover had a special log that was very special to him.
Rover's owner was a girl and her name was Kim,
She used to say to all the children, 'Come in.'

The children used to help Kim,
For example they used to feed him.
Rover loved the children being there,
They're were such a great pair.

Laura Tyther (10)
St Agnes RC Primary School

What Is Red?

Red is a fire engine
that drives to a fire.
Red is a robin
that you see on a tree.
Red is a lipstick
that the girls put on.
Red is a sofa
that you sit on to watch TV.
Red is a rose
that you give to a special person.
Red is a heart
that is full of blood.
Where would we be without the colour red?

Joseph Badr (7)
St Agnes RC Primary School

What Is Red?

Red is a new car
that is shiny and bright.
Red is a carpet
that never gets dirty.
Red is a lipstick
our mums wear all day.
Red is a robin
who likes to fly away.
Red is an apple
that is crunchy and nice.
Red is a heart
that beats in your body.
Red is a rose
a rose that you smell.
Red is a jumper you want to wear all night.
Where would we be without the colour red?

Laura Riddoch (6)
St Agnes RC Primary School

Squirrel

Squirrels are big,
Squirrels are small
They eat acorns
And also eat nuts.
Squirrels are bright
Squirrels are big fluffy things
They climb up trees and snooze all day.
While they make their winter nest way up in the tree
Where they store their acorns for the winter night
In the hole in the tree, that's where acorns lie.

Kathleen Street (10)
St Agnes RC Primary School

What Is Red?

Red is a red rose
that you can smell every day.

Red is a valentine heart
you give when it's Valentine's.

Red is blood
it comes when you have a cut.

Red is lipstick
that you put on your lips.

Red is a fire engine
that goes to people's fires.

Red is an apple
all crunchy and scrummy.

Where would we be without the colour red?

Gelsomina De Lucia (7)
St Agnes RC Primary School

The Snow

Snow is a little angel,
    falling from Heaven and lands on our heads.
It's like a paper ball
    dropped down the drain.
Everyone likes it
    People play snowball fights with their friends
and they have good fun too.
    It's a bit dangerous when cars are
driving or people are walking on it. When it melts it
    turns to ice
because it's so cold.

Tom Hand (9)
St Agnes RC Primary School

What Is A Rainbow?

It is different colours of stars in the sky
It is seven colours scattered in the air
Carved and wonderful
It is Christmas lights shining in the sky
It is the rain and the sun shining
The different colours of the sun
Different colours of lines to make the rainbow different
Ink of fountain pens scattered in the air.

George Osadebay (9)
St Agnes RC Primary School

My Best Poem

I am like a little helping hand because I am kind.
I am like a box of chocolates because I am lovely.
I am like a dog because I am excited.
I am like a teddy bear because I am cuddly.
I am like a flower, because I am kind.

Rebecca Whelan (6)
St Agnes RC Primary School

What Is The . . . Moon?

It is a torch shining
on a black piece of paper,
It is a candlelight
for everyone to see.
It is silver balloons
floating into the sky.
It is lots of doves
flying in harmony.
It is a Christmas bauble
twinkling in the sky.

Hayley McCafferty (10)
St Agnes RC Primary School

The Poem

I am like a teddy bear
Because I am cuddly.
I am like a dog
Because I am ready to catch the ball.
I am like a marshmallow
Because I am squishy.
I am like a cheetah
Because I can run fast.
I am like a lion,
Because I can roar really loud.
I am like a rabbit,
Because I love to eat carrots.
I am like a pencil,
Because I am a good writer.
I am like a door,
Because I am open.

Shane O'Gorman (6)
St Agnes RC Primary School

Is A Rainbow This Or Is It That?

A rainbow is dazzling coloured glitter stuck to
    the sky.
A rainbow is a pack of colouring pencils
    in the sky.
A rainbow is a lot of graceful ribbons flowing
    through the air.
A rainbow is some coloured paper fixed to the sky.
A rainbow is a flood of colours from out of the air.
A rainbow is coloured strips of sky made
    visible after a shower of rain.
A rainbow is a wonderful glow of radiant colours.
A rainbow is colours painted on the sky.

Siobhan Cloran (10)
St Agnes RC Primary School

What Is Snow?

Snow is a feather
    coming out of Jesus' pillow.
Snow is clouds melting
    from the sky then falling on our heads.
Snow is a star falling out of space.
Snow is ice cream
    falling from the sky.

Daniele Ignazi (9)
St Agnes RC Primary School

What Is The Rainbow?

It is seven beautiful colours,
    gleaming and glistening for everyone to see.
An artist's picture,
    shining in the gallery.
It is a surprise,
    to shock us all.
It is all the glitter in the world
    twinkling to make us gasp.
It is a crescent moon,
    sparkling on a rainy and sunny day.

Jessica Nock (9)
St Agnes RC Primary School

I Am Like . . .

I am like a little friend,
Because I am nice and kind.
I am like a big hug,
Because I am good.
I am like sleepovers,
Because I am exciting.
I am like a seed that won't grow,
Because I am sad.

Kofo Williams (6)
St Agnes RC Primary School

The Children

In come the children two by two
One with green eyes and one with blue.

In come the children three by three
Two are OK and one hurt their knee.

In come the children four by four
Two brought their mums and two run indoors.

In come the children five by five
Three like trees and two like hives.

In come the children six by six
Three play with babies and three play with sticks.

Monika D'Alessio (7)
St Agnes RC Primary School

Rabbits

Rabbits hop
Rabbits munch
Rabbits jump
And eat their lunch.

Steven Linacre (5)
St Agnes RC Primary School

The Babies

In come the babies two by two.
One with nappies and one called Sue.

In come the babies three by three
Two with black eyes and one with green.

In come the babies four by four
Two through the window and two through the door.

In come the babies five by five
Three are banging and scratching with knives.

Daniella Ekundayo (7)
St Agnes RC Primary School

What Is Red?

Red is a bow
that you put in your hair.
Red is a robin
that eats worms at Christmas.
Red is a fire engine
that put the fire out quickly.
Red is a dress
you wear at a party.
Red is blood
that's in your body.
Red is a rose
that pricks your fingers.
Red is an apple
all crunchy and scrummy.
Red is lipstick
that ladies wear.
Red is a postbox
that you put letters in.
Red is the sunset
that comes out in the evening.
Red is a bike
that you ride in the park.
What would we do without red?

Kieran Abbott (7)
St Agnes RC Primary School

All The Stuff I Do

I am like my dad,
Because I am handsome.
I am like a rocket,
Because I am loud.
I am like a motorbike,
Because I am cool.
I am like a phone,
Because I am loud.

Bopski Mbadiwe (6)
St Agnes RC Primary School

What Is Red?

Red is a red rose
that is beautiful.

Red is a bus
that is a double-decker bus.

Red is blood
that is in your body.

Red is a frog
that is very dangerous.

Red is a car
that you drive fast.

Where would we be without the colour red?

Joseph White (7)
St Agnes RC Primary School

Snow

Snow is falling from the skies,
I just can't believe my eyes!

I made a great snow angel on the ground,
The snow makes a funny crunching sound.

Snowballs are round and white,
My neighbour's got one, let's have a fight!

I made a snowman with a carrot for a nose,
My mum's taking a picture, I have to pose!

Snow is very hard and cold,
Do you know it's not hard to mould!

I wished and hoped this day would come,
Guess what? It's just begun!

Megan Abbott (10)
St Agnes RC Primary School

Animal World

When I go to my room and sit on my bed,
Something amazing comes into my head,
Instead of my room an animal world,
Then my imagination spins like a twirl.

Fascinating animals catch my sight,
My eyes glistening like a star so bright,
Pets or wild, I love them all,
Fat or thin, big or small.

Eating, drinking,
Playing, thinking,
Hunting, sleeping,
Crawling, creeping.

Cats scratching trees,
Wolves eating bees.
Dogs flicking fleas,
An elephant coming to sit on me!

When I leave my room after getting off my bed,
Something that was in, has left my head.

Amaka Enenmoh (11)
St Agnes RC Primary School

The Little Funny Poem

I am like a clown
Because I am funny.
I am like a happy face
Because I am kind.
I am like my bunk beds
Because I am excited.
I am like a teddy bear
Because I am cuddly.
I am like the sun
Because I am bright.

Eleanor Smith (6)
St Agnes RC Primary School

In The Dark Scaredy Kat!

'Night Kat.'
The room went pitch-black.
Shadows began to creep,
All, but me fell fast asleep.

I looked out my window,
The moon glared back with an eerie glow,
As the moon cast light silver,
Down my back ran a cold shiver.

Leering over my shed was my garden green
Suddenly a shadow witch grabbed me.
I ran to my mum's bed, tripping over my bedroom bin,
'Please Mum can I come in?'

Claire Gamble (11)
St Agnes RC Primary School

What I Am Like

I am like a dog waiting to go for a walk,
Because I am excited.
I am like a teddy bear,
Because I am kind.
I am like a funny clown
Because I can make everybody in yellow class laugh.
I am like a friend because I am happy.
I am like a cheetah
Because I can run, really, really fast.
I am like a lion,
Because I can roar really, really loud.
I am like a radio
Because I am really noisy.

Daniela Massaro (6)
St Agnes RC Primary School

I Am Like . . .

I am like a soft teddy,
Because I am happy.
I am like waking up,
Because I am excited.
I am like a teacher,
Because I am helpful.
I am like an elephant,
Because I am nosy.

Tiffany Godfrey (7)
St Agnes RC Primary School

Snakes

Snakes slither
Snakes slide
Snakes go ssss
Snakes hide.

Callum Murray (5)
St Agnes RC Primary School

I Am Like A . . .

I am like my dad
Because I am funny.
I am like a paintbrush
Because I am an artist.
I am like a friend smiling
Because I am a good boy.
I am like a monkey
Because I can climb trees.
I am like a cheetah
Because I can run fast.
I am like a clown
Because I make people laugh.

Roberto Evangelista (6)
St Agnes RC Primary School

What I Am Like . . .

I am like a star
Because I am one.
I am like a sun
Because I am happy.
I am like the moon
Because I am friendly.
I am like a rock
Because I am a bit tough.
I am like a box
Because I am hard.

Sebastian Tuck (6)
St Agnes RC Primary School

My Poem

I am like a teddy
Because I am happy.
I am like a smiley face
Because I am laughing.
I am like a dog waiting to go for a walk,
Because I am excited.

Adam Clark (6)
St Agnes RC Primary School

What I Am Like

I am like a smiley face
Because I am happy.
I am like a teddy bear
Because I am shiny.
I am like a clown,
Because I am funny.
I am like a radio,
Because I am loud.

Ciara McAndrew (6)
St Agnes RC Primary School

Look How I Am

I am like a flower,
because I am kind.
I am like a dog waiting to go for a walk,
because I am happy.
I am like my pet cat,
because I am cuddly.
I am like the stars,
because I am friendly.
I am like a clown,
because I am funny.

Anthony Rogal (6)
St Agnes RC Primary School

Snakes

Snakes slither,
Snakes bite,
Snakes give me
An awful fright!

Arthur Tyther (5)
St Agnes RC Primary School

The Big Poem

I am like Peter Bradley
because I am handsome.
I am like a computer
because I am happy.
I am like a dog
because I am kind.
I am like St Agnes School
because I am good.
I am like a hedgehog
because I am spiky.

Taylor Vigano (6)
St Agnes RC Primary School

Dogs

Dogs are big,
Dogs are small,
Dogs are furry,
And chase a ball.

Dogs can bark,
Dogs can run,
Dogs can chase,
Dogs are fun.

Anthonia Bosah (5)
St Agnes RC Primary School

My Kangaroo Haiku

My kangaroo hopped
With his two small legs over
He made me jump up!

Aljan Idrissov (5)
St Agnes RC Primary School

Dogs

Dogs eat bones
Dogs drink water
Dogs chase cats
Dogs eat tortoise.

Dogs are brown
Dogs are pink
Dogs are white
And they stink.

Lily Korenhof (5)
St Agnes RC Primary School

What's It Like To Be An Animal In The Jungle?

What's it like to be a roaring lion?
What's it like to be a snoring tiger?
What's it like to be a bouncy kangaroo?
What's it like to be a crocodile with the flu?
What's it like to be a hissing snake?
What's it like to be a giggling hyena?
What's it like to be a jumpy zebra?
What's it like to be a grumpy elephant?

What is it like to be an animal in the jungle?
I guess I'll never know.

Nana Esi Asabea Opoku-Adjei (11)
St Agnes RC Primary School

Dogs

Dogs eat
Dogs bite
Dogs eat rats
Dogs chase mice.

Jenny McCarthy (5)
St Agnes RC Primary School

Animal Poem

Cheetah running through the plains,
Tortoise taking step by step again and again,
Lion lying under the trees in the shade,
Chameleon lying on a rock, beginning to fade,
Little fish swimming in a stream,
Sloths hanging on trees having dreams,
Big blue whales in the deep sea,
Which one's my favourite? Don't ask me!

Chris Nealon (11)
St Agnes RC Primary School

I Am Like A Clown

I am like people in yellow class,
Because I am nice.
I am like a clown,
Because I am funny.
I am like a bear,
Because I am cuddly.
I am like a colourful classroom,
Because I am an artist.
I am like a TV,
Because I am entertaining.

Jovelito R Suniga Jnr (6)
St Agnes RC Primary School

Foxes

Foxes are red
Foxes eat mice
Foxes are furry
Foxes are nice.

Christopher Osadebay (5)
St Agnes RC Primary School

I Am Like . . .

I am like playing outside,
Because I am happy.
I am like a teddy,
Because I am soft.
I am like toys,
Because I am lovely.
I am like a maths problem,
Because I can be difficult.
I am like a maths problem
Because I am hardworking.

James Gruy (6)
St Agnes RC Primary School

What Is Red?

Red is a toy car that you get for Christmas.
Red is our heart that holds our love.
Red is a tomato with pips inside.
Red is a bouncy ball that bounces every day.
Red is a double-decker bus which carries people.
Red is the sun that you see in the morning.
What would we do without red?

Brandon Roberts (7)
St Agnes RC Primary School

Cats

Cats have fur
Cats chase mice
Cats can purr
And it's nice.

Nell Regan (5)
St Agnes RC Primary School

The Moon

While I was watching the moon one night,
I had a tremendous fright.
For there smiling back at me, the moon was staring straight at me!
The beautiful yellow moon shone brightly in the sky,
Honestly I thought I was going to cry,
So beautiful, so bright, the most fantastic sight.
So there and then I rested my head,
With the moon guarding over my bed.

Clare Hand (11)
St Agnes RC Primary School

Goblin

Cautiously, quietly,
and alert for danger.
It has good sense of direction,
like a forest ranger.

With sharp claws,
and red blood eyes,
during the night
it howls and cries.

Greedy, selfish,
and it loves its food
and especially
when it's in a mood.

Jamie Harkin (11)
St Agnes RC Primary School

What Is Red?

Red is blood,
When you cut your hand.

Red is a heart
When you kiss the girls.

Red is a robin
That flies in the sky.

Red is an apple
That you eat.

Red is a pencil
You write with.

Eris Herbert (7)
St Agnes RC Primary School

Animals

I love my little bunny rabbit,
But oh, he has a dreadful habit,
Of paddling among the rocks,
And soaking both his bunny socks.

I love my little baby bear,
I love his nose and toes and hair.
I like to hold him in my arms,
And keep him away from harm.

I love my furry little cat,
I love his colourful sleeping mat,
His lovely mat is made of silk,
I like it when he purrs for milk.

Isabel Foulsham (10)
St Agnes RC Primary School

Don't Feed The Animals!

Don't feed the animals, you might get a fright,
Don't feed the animals, you might get a bite.
The zookeeper says, 'Come and see but don't touch.'
I didn't like the snakes very much!

I saw a tiger who leap-frogged another,
It growled and snarled and sniffed at my brother.
We turned and ran back to the shop,
Now I prefer animals that hop!

Bismark Bisquera (11)
St Agnes RC Primary School

My Trampoline

Bounce, bounce
As high as I can go
Up to the clouds
And down I go.

My friends come round
And all join in
Up we bop and down again.

Backward flips and belly dips
'This is great,' the girls scream
How they love my trampoline.

Francie Smyth (11)
St Agnes RC Primary School

My Dog

My dog is small
My dog is sweet
My dog means the world to me.

My dog can run
My dog can jump
Me and my dog have so much fun
My dog can bark
My dog loves to play in the park.

I love my dog and she loves me
Together we're the bestest friends there can be.

Claudine Kirby (11)
St Agnes RC Primary School

What Is Red?

Red is a clock
That goes tick-tock
Red is a bike
That you ride in the park
Red is a valentine card
That you give to your mummy
Red is a rose
That you see in your garden
Red is a car
That you play with at Christmas
Red is a bow
That you put in your hair
Red is an apple
That is juicy and crunchy
Where would we be without red?

Katy McLaughlin (7)
St Agnes RC Primary School

Rabbit

Rabbit sleeps in a hut
Rabbit goes to Pizza Hut
Rabbit shares with friends
Rabbit hops in the garden
Rabbit goes out with friends
Rabbit goes to Pizza Hut again
Rabbit says, 'Stop pulling my ears.'
Rabbit hops away.

Wyonna Loh (10)
St Agnes RC Primary School

What Is Red?

Red is a clock
that goes tick-tock.

Red is a robin
that is in a tree.

Red is a valentine's card
that you give to your mummy.

Red is an apple
all crunchy and yummy.

Red is a car
that is very sporty.

Where would we be without red?

Bridget Tighe (7)
St Agnes RC Primary School

What Is Red?

Red is a
heart that pumps your blood.
Red is a
robin that comes in winter.
Red is a
fire engine that goes to fires
Red is a
rose that is beautiful
Red is a
colour that I like.

Michael O'Connor (7)
St Agnes RC Primary School

What Is Red?

Red is a rose
that you give to your mum
Red is an apple
all juicy and crunchy
Red is a car
that goes very fast
Red is a sun
that you see in the morning
Red is a hat
that you wear to a wedding
Red is lipstick
that your mum wears
What would we do without the colour red?

Bruno Fernandes (7)
St Agnes RC Primary School

What Is Red?

Red is a rose
that you smell all day.

Red is a car
with four round wheels.

Red is a fire engine
when there is a fire.

Red is an apple
that is red and shiny.

Red is lipstick
that you put on your lips.

Where would we be without red?

Alexander Craig (7)
St Agnes RC Primary School

What is Red?

Red is a fast car
that you drive.

Red is a rose that you
give to your mummy.

Red is a woolly jumper
you wear when it's cold.

Red is a fire engine
that puts fires out.

Where would we be without red?

Grace Kelly (7)
St Agnes RC Primary School

What Is Red?

Red is a bow
That you wear on your hair
Red is a lipstick
That your mummy wears
Red is a car
That drives along the road
Red is an apple
You eat and it's yummy
Red is a square
Which has four sides
Red is a clock
And it goes tick-tock
Red is a pair of shoes
That are shiny and red
What would we do without the colour red?

Hugo Lopez (7)
St Agnes RC Primary School

The Story Of George

George was a silly boy
He ate some mould from his toy
And so he was told
Not to eat that ghastly mould.
And so he went back to bed
But in the morning he was dead.

Andrew Younger (8)
St Benedict's Junior School

Careful Of It!

I see a bright fish like light,
It swims around gliding in a tank,
It glides gracefully and quite quickly,
It's bright like light,
Its body is quite round and nice,
Its skin is smooth and beautiful,
It doesn't make a sound, it's peaceful,
If someone looks deeply at it it will look at you,
So beware of him he might make you
        Blind!

Daniel Gajkowski (9)
St Benedict's Junior School

Animal Poem

I see an enchanted elephant crashing
through the jumpy jungle clumsily.
Its skin is rougher than a revolting red roof
and kills every person in its way
with one . . . *stomp!*
It picks up things with its trunk like a tough
tiger one way or another.

Tito Simonelli (9)
St Benedict's Junior School

The Writer Of This Poem
(Based on 'The Writer of this Poem' by Roger McGough)

The writer of this poem is taller than a tree.
As strong as a wrestler
As gentle as a bee.

As fast as a rocket
As slow as a sock
As happy as a haggis
As silly as a rock.

As soppy as a Barbie
As lame as Action Man
As dead as an army
As the writer is me.

Harry McAdam (8)
St Benedict's Junior School

The Writer Of This Poem Is . . .
(Based on 'The Writer of this Poem' by Roger McGough)

As big as a house,
As strong as a cup winning weightlifter,
As gentle as a Barbie
As fast as a 400m sprinter,
As slow as a snail,
As happy as the dog in the Churchill advert,
As silly as a turnip,
As quick as Kieron Dyer,
As lame as Action Man,
As boring as a life story,
As dead as Hitler.

Robert Picheta (9)
St Benedict's Junior School

The Wolf Man

In the deep, deep woods
The wolf man lurks
In the tall, tall trees
The wolf man lives.

'Don't go there that's
Where the wolf man lives.
He will kill you.'

The warrior draws
His trusty sword and
Stood still until . . .
Pounce, the wolf man strikes.

The warrior fell with
A loud smack and died.

Aran Clifford (8)
St Benedict's Junior School

Crabs

I see a red, nasty crab
Nipping at my toes, sideways he goes.
Colouring - orange, blurry red,
And this is what he said,
'I'm a thin crab, you're not.
I'm a fast crab, you're not.
I have a shell, you haven't.'
It said in a cracky voice.
And at that moment
He was gobbled up by a seagull.

Daniel Angwin (9)
St Benedict's Junior School

Kings 33 Miles Apart

Who would have thought near Sutton Hoo
We would have found not one but two
Grand Anglo-Saxon British kings
Buried in graves with their fine things.

With jewellery of silver and gold
Which once were new but now are old.
The weapons found show they were brave
Was it war which led them to the grave?

One lies at Sutton Hoo
The other at South End
Were they strangers,
Enemies or friends?

When I grow up I'd like to find
The answers to these riddles strange
And study history and help our minds
To open and to change.

Joe Clift (8)
St Gildas' RC Junior School

My Bedroom

M y bedroom can be messy
Y ou would think I should try harder.

B ut my toys are loved and cared for
E ver so soft and happy to see me
D reams - some scary some nice
R over my dog doesn't help that much
O ver the bed he chases my toy mice
O n Saturday it's tidy up day
M um says, 'If it's all done, you can go out to play.'

Caitriona Quinlan (9)
St Gildas' RC Junior School

If I Were Born On Valentine's Day

If I were born on Valentine's Day
My heart would be filled with love
I would shout out loud to Cupid,
And he would fly down from above.

I would give him a wish list
Of all the things I would like to have
And I'd hope he'd give them all to me
Because he knows I would be glad.

I would ask for lots of chocolates
Balloons, a card and cake
But most of all I'd ask to see
Justin Timberlake.

I'd ask him to come to St Gildas'
To perform some of his songs
And at the end of his concert
He'd ask me to sing along.

If I were born on Valentine's Day
It would be lots of fun
To have Justin Timberlake sing to me
In front of everyone.

Monét Boyce-Nelson (9)
St Gildas' RC Junior School

Relaxation

When I throw a stone
I realised it shone
But it was not in Rome
It was just back at home.

It was not for attraction
It was for good action
But when it comes to relaxation
My mind is out of this nation.

Esteban Lanao (8)
St Gildas' RC Junior School

Football Is The Best

Football is the best,
It's much better than all the rest.
Once I played hockey,
Then I wanted to be a jockey,
But football is still the best.

I tried to play rugby
But the players are too rough for me.
Jonny Wilkinson is a big man,
I think I'm his biggest fan,
But football is still the best.

Basketball is alright but sometimes the players fight.
When I tried to play pool
I just looked like a fool,
But football is still the very best
I love it more than all the rest.

Taetum Lyons (9)
St Gildas' RC Junior School

All About Summer

The sky is clear,
The sun is shining,
The grass is green,
And everyone's smiling.
Why oh why, it is a beautiful day,
Why oh why do people cry and get angry
Because the sun is shining?
Why oh why in Dublin is it cold
And why can't it shine?
Why oh why
What wonderful teachers
We have to learn with.

Shane Scott (8)
St Gildas' RC Junior School

Sailing Boat By A Sea And Mountains

The smiling sun looks down at the mysterious waters below it,
which wave to the ragged rocks which stand unmovable.
The cypress tree makes way for the light blue sky above
as the menacing mountains try to block it out and cast the
scene below into shadow.
The multicoloured sailing boat drifts silently on the tide.

The glistening sun gazes at the fiery-coloured sand on which the
hairy grass is blown silently in the wind,
the dark blue waters gleam, concealing their secrets far beneath.
The clouds swirl round in the sky, dancing around the orange
ball of flame.

The mountains lie in the background, biding their time.
They wait for the opportunity to shield the sun from view for
them to bask in.
They glare at the trees which allow the kindly sun to share its
light and warmth.

Sunshine glances at the fine sands of the brilliant beach,
dazzling the fine blades of the mint-green grass.
Ragged rocks bury themselves further into the grounds,
the boat follows the waves, being guided as the sun
disappears beyond the horizon.

The mountains give in on their task to steal the sun and sit back,
resting up for another assault the following day.
The sands relax as the tide loses its strength as the sun tires
and leaves to rest before the next day where it will shine once again.

Andrew Dickson (10)
St Gildas' RC Junior School

Football Is . . .

Football is about playing with friends
Football is scoring and winning
Football is about kicking your ball
Football is about having fun.

Timothy Peters (8)
St Gildas' RC Junior School

Miss O'Donnell Thinks I'm Reading But I'm . . .

Miss O'Donnell thinks I'm reading but I'm . . .
Standing on top of the big rock
Drinking a view of the sea
Sailing a ship to dry land
In fact I'm not at school at all.

Miss O'Donnell thinks I'm reading but I'm . . .
Singing on Top of the Pops
Playing the piano with Elton John
Dancing with Michael Jackson
In fact I'm not at school at all.

Miss O'Donnell thinks I'm reading but I'm . . .
Swimming with dolphins
But I am feeding sharks
Sailing the oceans
In fact I'm not at school at all.

Miss O'Donnell thinks I'm reading but I'm . . .
Playing a computer
Singing through the dark
In fact I'm not at school at all.

Samantha Scott (10)
St Gildas' RC Junior School

Guess Which Fruit

Red or green but always round,
Grows in orchards, not on the ground,
Juicy and handy, smooth and ripe,
Crunchy, delicious, lots of different types,
Full of vitamins, good for you
They even help you go to the loo!

Tina Marfo Ruth (8)
St Gildas' RC Junior School

Miss O'Donnell Thinks I'm Reading But I'm . . .

Miss O'Donnell thinks I'm reading but I'm . . .
Gliding over the Amazon, trekking through the dangerous rainforest,
scuttling away from a black jaguar
in fact I'm not in school at all.

Miss O'Donnell thinks I'm reading but I'm . . .
Scanning the seabed, stroking the smooth skin of a whale,
riding on a sea horse's back
in fact I'm not at school at all.

Miss O'Donnell thinks I'm reading but I'm . . .
Surfing the Milky Way, gazing at the stars lit up like the morning sun,
spinning on Saturn's rings
in fact I'm not in school at all.

Miss O'Donnell thinks I'm reading but I'm . . .
Admiring Mount Everest, abseiling from the summit,
gazing at the cities below
in fact I'm not in school at all.

Miss O'Donnell thinks I'm reading but I'm . . .
Gliding over the Amazon, trekking through the dangerous rainforest
scuttling away from a black jaguar
in fact I'm not at school at all.

Kitty Lees-Edmondson (10)
St Gildas' RC Junior School

Bumpus Jumpus Dinosaumpus!

There's a quake and a quiver and a rumbling around
It makes you shiver.
It's a thundery sound,
Shake, shake, shudder . . .
Near the sludgy old swamp.
The dinosaurs are coming
And are ready to romp.

Connor Westbrook (9)
St Gildas' RC Junior School

Miss O'Donnell Thinks I'm Reading

Miss O'Donnell thinks I'm reading but I'm . . .
Swimming in the deep blue sea, sailing on the waves,
Tackling rapids in a wooden canoe
In fact I'm not at school at all.

Miss O'Donnell thinks I'm reading but I'm . . .
Dancing in the moonlight,
Watching the silver stars,
Hearing palm trees rustle,
In fact I'm not at school at all.

Miss O'Donnell thinks I'm reading but I'm . . .
Travelling into space, watching all the planets spin,
Sitting on Jupiter
In fact I'm not at school at all.

Miss O'Donnell thinks I'm reading but I'm . . .
Swimming the deep blue sea, sailing on the waves
Tackling rapids in a wooden canoe
In fact I'm not at school at all.

Tamara Prince-Gabb (10)
St Gildas' RC Junior School

Blue

Blue is the colour of the sky
Blue is up so high
Blue is the colour of my ruler
Blue are the eyes of Nuala
Blue is the colour of bluebell
Blue is the colour of water wells
Blue is the colour of the farmer's hat
Blue is the colour of my cat!

Nuala Reidy (8)
St Gildas' RC Junior School

My Class A - O

A is for Aaron, who has red hair
B is for Bonnie, who likes Elvis
C is for Christian, who loves yoga
D is for Dalia, who is pretty as can be
E is for Elise, who is a groovy chick
F is for Filipe, who likes the colour blue
G is for all the girls, who run around and play
H is for Henry, who is smart as smart can be
I is for ink, which we use for our pens
J is for Joseph, who likes to sit and read
K is for Kyle, who is very funny
L is for Linda, that is our teacher's name!
M is for Mia, who is best friends with Tillie
N is for Nadia, who is very sensible
O is for the odd thing, lying on the floor.

Elise McNamara (9)
St Gildas' RC Junior School

Miss O'Donnell Thinks I'm Reading But I'm . . .

Miss O'Donnell thinks I'm reading but I'm . . .
Travelling into space, in a rainforest looking for a parrot,
Climbing up mountains
In fact I'm not at school at all.

Miss O'Donnell thinks I'm reading but I'm . . .
Helping the poor with Jesus in the sky
Nursing the sick, helping the down-hearted
In fact I'm not at school at all.

Miss O'Donnell thinks I'm reading but I'm . . .
Starring in a film with Arnold, racing Leonardo di Caprio,
Playing basketball with Philip
In fact I'm not at school at all.

Luke Scott (11)
St Gildas' RC Junior School

Talents

A is for Anna who is very rude
B is for Ben, well he thinks he's a dude
C is for Clover, she is funny
D is for Dalia who loves money
E is for Elise, she's my best friend
F is for Fred who likes to pretend
G is for George, he's a pain
H is for Henry who made up a game
I is for Icole who likes to draw
J is for Jack who wants more, more, more
K is for Kyra who loves school
L is for Leila who loves the swimming pool
M is for Mia who loves to sing
N is for Nadia who hates the sound
O is for Olly, he loves to eat
P is for Peter who prefers the name Pete
Q is for Quelyn who acts like a pig
R is for Rhianne who loves to dig
S is for Shannah who paddles in bogs
T is for Tillie who loves dogs
U is for Ursular who's on TV
V is for Vera who wants to make all
W is for Woody who hates showers
X is for Xoya who loves flowers
Y is for Yichmin who's favourite word's well
Z is for Zara who loves to tell.

Bonnie Benoiton (8)
St Gildas' RC Junior School

What Is A Star?

A star is a glowing rock floating up so very high,
A golden diamond pasted in the dark night sky.
Drifting in the sea of tranquility with no sound at all,
When the sun lights up the sky, it's time to say goodbye!

Anthony Graham-Dillon (9)
St Gildas' RC Junior School

Miss O'Donnell Thinks I'm Reading

Miss O'Donnell thinks I'm reading but I'm . . .
Flying the last Concorde, driving a race car at 100mph,
Riding a roller coaster round and round,
In fact I'm not at school at all.

Miss O'Donnell thinks I'm reading but I'm . . .
Starring in a Shakespeare play, singing in a West End musical,
Writing a best seller with J K Rowling,
In fact I'm not at school at all.

Miss O'Donnell thinks I'm reading but I'm . . .
Shooting at aliens on Mars, orbiting Jupiter in a solar-powered rocket,
Rocking around in an asteroid belt,
In fact I'm not at school at all.

Miss O'Donnell thinks I'm reading but I'm . . .
Running a marathon with Paula Radcliffe, riding the winning horse
                                        in the Grand National,
Soring a goal for Arsenal FC,
I fact I'm not at school at all.

Miss O'Donnell thinks I'm reading but I'm . . .
Flying the last Concorde, driving a race car at 100mph,
Riding a roller coaster round and round,
In fact I'm not at school at all.

Evelyn Gompertz (10)
St Gildas' RC Junior School

Mother

My mum is good at cooking
On Monday she takes me to school
Thank you for making my mum
Her care is so good to me
Everyone's mum is special to them
Roses are my mum's favourite flowers.

Dalia Striganaviciute (8)
St Gildas' RC Junior School

Snowflakes

Snowflakes falling
Dripping and dropping
It is pouring
Gladly not raining.

I am covered in snow
And so is my little red bow
My friend was feeling low
So I gave her the red bow.

We played snowball fights
So I had to pull up my woolly tights
It started to rain
Oh boy! What a pain.

It poured and poured
It dripped and dropped
It wasn't hot
And I never got to see the snow a lot.

Shannah McGauran (8)
St Gildas' RC Junior School

In Kyle's Drawer

In Kyle's drawer he keeps . . .
Ten sets of paints
Nine Game Boys
Eight Beyblades
Seven sets of T-shirts
Six sets of trousers
Five sets of shorts
Four mouldy, squashed oranges
Three smelly, wet socks
Two Arsenal kits
One and . . . *himself.*

Kyle Joseph (9)
St Gildas' RC Junior School

Miss O'Donnell Thinks I'm Reading

Miss O'Donnell thinks I'm reading but I'm . . .
Travelling to the warm and sandy beach, flying through the
cloudless sky, climbing on the rocky mountains.
In fact I'm not at school at all.

Miss O'Donnell thinks I'm reading but I'm . . .
Swimming in the deep blue ocean, making a big castle in the sand,
sailing in the River Severn.
In fact I'm not at school at all.

Miss O'Donnell thinks I'm reading but I'm . . .
Swimming and gazing at the stars in the dark sky, diving in
the tropical sea, playing with a brown monkey in the jungle.
In fact I'm not at school at all.

Miss O'Donnell thinks I'm reading but I'm . . .
Travelling to the warm and sandy beach, flying through the
cloudless sky, climbing on the rocky mountains.
In fact I'm not at school at all.

Anita Gmiat (11)
St Gildas' RC Junior School

My Rabbit

I love my rabbit
She is very cute, she loves it when I play the flute
She wiggles her ears when I tickle her toes
And has a very pink nose.
She cuddles up to me and
She feels very warm, especially when she eats corn.
She loves her treat and when she is tickled she is so, so, so sweet.
My rabbit is called Sue and you know what?
She loves me too!

Shannon Bono (8)
St Gildas' RC Junior School

Starry Night

The vast mountains are towering and protecting the cluttered village.

The tree is lofty and thin and looks like flames of fire,
Swaying from side to side in the moonlit sky.

The stars are glistening up high in a dark, deep sea,
Lighting the wintry village and keeping it bright.

The cosy, warm cottages emanate their friendly shining lights.

The swirling wind is swaying across the sky,
Around the glittering stars and over the crescent moon,
Making whirls and curls high above.

A glowing, golden moon is suspended in the darkness,
Lighting up the peaceful village and the midnight sky.

Elizabeth Demetriou (10)
St Gildas' RC Junior School

When School Assembly Was Finished

Miss Carr's lot were towed out
Mr Volcano's class burst out,
Mrs Olympics lot raced out,
Miss Vomit's class . . . vomited.

Miss Flower's lot . . . rose,
Mrs Quiet's class did not make a sound,
Mr Crazy's class psyched out,
Mr Gun's lot shot off,
But
Mrs Invisible's class
Just vanished!

Rhianne Burnett (9)
St Gildas' RC Junior School

Miss O'Donnell Thinks I'm Reading

Miss O'Donnell thinks I'm reading but I'm . . .
Exploring the deep blue sea, discovering the world of Atlantis,
uncovering new underwater creatures,
in fact I'm not at school at all.

Miss O'Donnell thinks I'm reading but I'm . . .
Visiting the Ice Age, meeting the Egyptians, travelling with
the Romans,
in fact I'm not at school at all.

Miss O'Donnell thinks I'm reading but I'm . . .
Cycling through the finish line, winning the silver cup
for running, gaining a personal record for swimming,
in fact I'm not at school at all.

Miss O'Donnell thinks I'm reading but I'm . . .
Walking through the Eiffel Tower, climbing up Mount Everest,
taking photos of the Statue of Liberty,
in fact I'm not at school at all.

Miss O'Donnell thinks I'm reading but I'm . . .
Exploring the deep blue sea, discovering the world of Atlantis,
uncovering new underwater creatures,
in fact I'm not at school at all.

Rowena Bicknell (11)
St Gildas' RC Junior School

What Is The Sea?

The ferocious sea is like a footballer tackling the keeper roughly
and getting sent off.
It is like a herd of charging horses galloping competitively to the end.
The sea is like a playful pack of lion cubs fighting mischievously
together.
It looks like a blue crashing shield that protects the whole world.
It can be as calm as a quiet and forgotten street.

Lamar Esty (9)
St Gildas' RC Junior School

Miss O'Donnell Thinks I'm Reading

Miss O'Donnell thinks I'm reading but I'm . . .
Gazing at the gleaming stars, flying up into space,
dancing in the moonlight,
in fact I'm not at school at all.

Miss O'Donnell thinks I'm reading but I'm . . .
surfing on a beach in Barbados, watching sunset fall,
hearing the sea sway,
in fact I'm not at school at all.

Miss O'Donnell thinks I'm reading but I'm
climbing Mount Everest, sailing the Pacific Ocean,
skiing down a hill,
in fact I'm not at school at all.

Miss O'Donnell thinks I'm reading but I'm . . .
Gazing at the gleaming stars, flying up into space,
dancing in the moonlight
in fact I'm not at school at all.

Taylor Kershaw (11)
St Gildas' RC Junior School

What Is The Night?

The night is a black ghost
Flying across the night sky,
Leaving its laugh echoing behind it.
The night is like millions of black bats,
Crows and ravens all stuck together,
Not moving,
Not even a blink or a wink,
Just all the time sleeping.

Jagoda Lisiecka (10)
St Gildas' RC Junior School

Miss O'Donnell Thinks I'm Reading

Miss O'Donnell thinks I'm reading but I'm . . .
Winning the FA Cup with Arsenal, kicking a penalty for
                                            Castleford Tigers,
Scoring a goal against Michael Jordan,
In fact I'm not at school at all.

Miss O'Donnell thinks I'm reading but I'm . . .
Starring in 'Titanic', singing with R Kelly in the studio,
Practising my skills with Thierry Henry,
In fact I'm not at school at all.

Miss O'Donnell thinks I'm reading but I'm . . .
Swimming through the waves in the ocean, booting a ball
                                            in the air,
Climbing on the icy mountains,
In fact I'm not at school at all.

Miss O'Donnell thinks I'm reading but I'm . . .
Playing with the dolphins, feeding the fishes,
Glaring as the sharks are snapping past,
In fact I'm not at school at all.

Miss O'Donnell thinks I'm reading but I'm . . .
Swinging in space, flying over the sunny beach,
Jumping off a tall building,
In fact I'm not at school at all.

Miss O'Donnell thinks I'm reading but I'm . . .
Wrestling with the lions, hunting the wolves down,
Racing with the cheetahs,
In fact I'm not at school at all.

Konnell Vassell (10)
St Gildas' RC Junior School

Miss O'Donnell Thinks I'm Reading

Miss O'Donnell thinks I'm reading but I'm . . .
swimming with dolphins, feeding the sharks,
gazing at fish, as they swim by,
in fact I'm not at school at all.

Miss O'Donnell thinks I'm reading but I'm . . .
posing for Vogue walking down the catwalk in
designer clothes, being interviewed by presenters,
in fact I'm not at school at all.

Miss O'Donnell thinks I'm reading but I'm . . .
making new CDs with lots of celebrities,
signing autographs for my fans,
receiving an award for Best Album of the Year,
in fact I'm not at school at all.

Miss O'Donnell thinks I'm reading but I'm . . .
digging underground for lost treasure,
trying to find lots of gold, going to be rich,
in fact I'm not at school at all.

Miss O'Donnell thinks I'm reading but I'm . . .
waterskiing on an exotic holiday,
enjoying the sun and gushing through the cool blue sea,
in fact I'm not at school at all.

Miss O'Donnell thinks I'm reading but I'm . . .
swimming with dolphins, feeding the sharks,
gazing at fish as they swim by,
in fact I'm not at school at all.

Wendy Shoniregun (11)
St Gildas' RC Junior School

Miss O'Donnell Thinks I'm Reading

Miss O'Donnell thinks I'm reading but I'm . . .
Climbing up on the rocky mountain,
Feeling snow dropping on my nose,
Slipping on the ice,
In fact I am not at school at all.

Miss O'Donnell thinks I'm reading but I'm . . .
Swimming under the dark blue water,
Floating above the wavy ocean,
Diving in the green and blue river,
In fact I am not at school at all.

Miss O'Donnell thinks I'm reading but I'm . . .
In space exploring, floating above the planet Saturn,
I am sitting on the earth gazing at the stars,
In fact I am not at school at all.

Miss O'Donnell thinks I'm reading but I'm . . .
Running in the forest that's dark and damp,
Jumping on the lily pad,
Speaking to the furry animals,
In fact I am not at school at all.

Miss O'Donnell thinks I'm reading but I'm . . .
Climbing up on the rocky mountain,
Feeling snow dropping on my nose,
Slipping on the ice,
In fact I am not at school at all.

Shauna Davis
St Gildas' RC Junior School

What Is The Sea?

The sea is like a pair of snatching hands pulling you into the deep.
It is like my brother storming up the stairs like an eagle.
The sea is like two people arguing viciously and yelling at each other.
It is a lion roaring to scare you away.
The sea is like a stampede of elephants running through the jungle.

Conor O'Leary (9)
St Gildas' RC Junior School

Miss O'Donnell

Miss O'Donnell thinks I'm reading but I'm . . .
Watching the palm trees sway,
dancing under the moonlight in Barbados, lying on the sandy beach,
in fact I'm not at school at all.

Miss O'Donnell thinks I'm reading but I'm . . .
Sailing on the biggest ocean,
gazing at the blue sky, watching the waves clash
in fact I'm not at school at all.

Miss O'Donnell thinks I'm reading but I'm . . .
Flying over the dark blue ocean watching as dolphins glide
exploring the deserts, searching through the tombs,
in fact I'm not at school at all.

Miss O'Donnell thinks I'm reading but I'm . . .
At the summit of Snowdon,
admiring the view, knowing I am the youngest person
that climbed the mountain
in fact I'm not at school at all.

Miss O'Donnell thinks I'm reading but I'm . . .
Watching the palm trees sway,
dancing in the moonlight in Barbados, lying on the sandy beach,
in fact I'm not at school at all.

Louise Millar (10)
St Gildas' RC Junior School

What Is The Sea?

The sea is like a bristling bull running wildly.
It is like a raging avalanche tumbling recklessly down
                                        a vast valley.
It is like an underwater jungle with only colourful trees inside
                                  that are hiding creatures.
It is like a giant clapping his hands together and stamping his feet.

Temitope Smith-Quim (10)
St Gildas' RC Junior School

Miss O'Donnell Thinks I'm Reading

Miss O'Donnell thinks I'm reading but I'm . . .
Climbing on Mount Everest trembling with fear, swimming in
                                                    Niagara Falls,

Soaring high with the elegant doves,
In fact I'm not at school at all.

Miss O'Donnell thinks I'm reading but I'm . . .
Exploring the dangerous jungle, watching the butterflies flutter
                                                swiftly in the air,

Swimming with the hundreds of fishes in the sea,
In fact I'm not at school at all.

Miss O'Donnell thinks I'm reading but I'm . . .
Gazing at the stars, dancing in the twilight,
Watching the sun set on the horizon,
In fact I'm not at school at all.

Miss O'Donnell thinks I'm reading but I'm . . .
Exploring Pluto and Mars, discovering new life,
Landing in a new galaxy,
In fact I'm not at school at all.

Miss O'Donnell thinks I'm reading but I'm . . .
Climbing on Mount Everest trembling with fear, swimming in
                                                    Niagara Falls,

Soaring high with the elegant doves,
In fact I'm not at school at all.

Dominic Canokema Kuluba (11)
St Gildas' RC Junior School

What Is The Sea?

The sea is a hand trying to grab you anxiously with excitement.
The sea is a pouring tap that never ends and floods the Earth.
It is like my little cousin throwing a tantrum with my baby brother.
The sea is a blue blanket waving through the fresh, clean air.
It is powerful, like a huge army tank trampling over everything
                                                        in sight.

Marcus Amaral Arrais (10)
St Gildas' RC Junior School

What Is The Sea?

The sea is like a protective lioness chasing a hungry zebra
in the wild.
It is a magical door opening to a brand new world.
It is like a dolphin leaping in the dark seas at night.
It is like a teacher roaring at naughty children.
It is like my dad and I fighting like two lions, deep in the forest.
It is like a shiny mirror, where you can see yourself.

Catalina Ogilvie-Browne (9)
St Gildas' RC Junior School

What Is The Sea?

The sea is like a herd of horses galloping and leaping madly.
It is like my annoying brother and I squabbling with anger.
It is like glitter, flowing, spreading, shining with sparkles.
It is like another world, with twinkling creatures on a soft, sandy floor.
It can be dark and scary, like a bad dream.
The waves are like beautiful dolphins that come up and jump in
                                                                                             the sky.

Kadisha Knight (9)
St Gildas' RC Junior School

Starry Night

The swaying, green tree is pointing to far-off lands.
The glowing stars are scintillating and yellow.
The invisible wind is sinuous and strong.
The midnight sky is turning dark blue.
The crescent moon is shining like a blazing torch in a misty sky.
The bulky hill is as knobbly as a camel's humps.

Keith Adjei Twum Donker (10)
St Gildas' RC Junior School

Sailing Boat By A Sea And Mountains

The river moves backwards and forwards, it moves so calmly.
The blue sea moves between the sun and the trees.
The boat floats along the river that moves backwards and forwards.

The sun swirls around and around, as hot as a fireball.
The cypress tree springs upwards two by two,
It moves slowly in the smooth wind.

The rocks are rough like sandpaper to smooth out the sun.
The mountains are standing like stiff soldiers on parade.
The grass is like wildness rushing here and there.
The sand is like smoothing out a piece of wood with rough
                                                            sandpaper.

The waves of the sea move calmly like never before.
The wind is there so calmly, there is no movement.
Everything goes quiet and all the movements stop to watch us
                                              finish painting.
The painting is finished and it says bye-bye.

Rebecca Wilson (11)
St Gildas' RC Junior School

Ski, Ski, Ski

Ski, ski, ski till you freeze
In the cold morning breeze.
Ski, ski, ski down the slopes
With all of your fears and hopes.
Ski, ski, ski in the sun
Making sure you have lots of fun.
Ski, ski, ski day or night
I don't mind, I have no fright.
Ski, ski, ski in the snow
And I hope that it will never go.
         Ski, ski, ski.

Alexandra O'Keeffe (9)
St Gildas' RC Junior School

Sailing Boat By A Sea And Mountains

The vast sky is like a blue blanket pulled over by God,
With angels' wings holding it up.

The curving clouds dance through the sky,
Like fluffy, white sheep bouncing by.

The spiralling sun burst with colour,
It is impossible for it to get any duller.
The menacing mountains look down at all,
Extremely menacing and extremely tall.

The deep and mysterious sea is wondered by all,
Covered by its crystal clear shell.

The tall, green trees reach the sky
And wave at everyone who dares to walk by.

The ragged rocks get battered by the sea,
The sun and sky look down at this with glee.

The glistening sand sparkles and shimmers,
It gets happier and happier when the gentle tide tickles it.

The boat bobs up and down and winks,
With this stormy weather it is probably going to sink.

Aisling Quinlan (11)
St Gildas' RC Junior School

Winter Comes

Winter comes, cream frost and cold,
Snow is falling just like gold.

Autumn rises, winter goes,
Flowers rise, the smell of rose.

Trees are budding with green leaves,
Flowers are full of buzzy bees.

Collecting pollen for the summer,
Making the flowers fuller and fuller.

Niamh Byrne-Roberts (9)
St Gildas' RC Junior School

Sailing Boat By A Sea And Mountains

The sea smells of rapid fresh air
and has a dazzling colour of air and crystal blue;
the sea carries a boat,
making it drift through the water of mystery,
waiting to discover what is out there.
The mountain has no end to how high it goes
and only the most skilled and fearless men could climb it.
The shore lies for people to rest their sensitive heads
on the warm, soft sand,
which leads them to a dreamworld.
The cypress tree is a house of a wood elf
holding tons of magic to put upon people.
The sky holds many, many angels who protect us below
while we carry out our lives, playing out our role.
The sun has a cheerful face watching us all the time,
but soon the sun goes down.

Sean Crean (12)
St Gildas' RC Junior School

What Is The Sea?

The sea is a wild crowd of people,
Arguing madly all day and night.

It is waving non-stop like a fluffy, smooth duvet,
Lying on a bed.

It is like a magical door,
To a mysterious, unknown world.

It is a deserted, lonely forest,
Going deeper and deeper.

It is like a calm night,
With everyone sleeping soundly.

Dillon Cuffe (9)
St Gildas' RC Junior School

Henry VIII And His Six Wives

Henry VIII had a fat, fat face,
It was agony for him going at fast pace.

Catherine of Aragon was very nice,
Until she found out she had head lice.

Anne Boleyn was very fat-headed,
But in the end she got beheaded.

Jane Seymour gave birth to an heir,
But 12 days later she didn't leave a hair.

Anne of Cleves was the ugly one,
Sadly she did not give birth to a son.

Catherine Howard was substituted,
Then afterwards she was executed.

Katherine Parr was very nice,
Unfortunately she hated mice.

Marcos Fernandez (10)
St Gildas' RC Junior School

Starry Night

The moon was in the sky over the village.
The moon is like a fireball, swirling in the sky over the quiet village.
The tree is tall and thin.
The dark, trembling tree waved its branches in the wind.
The stars are shiny.
The twinkling stars sparkled like silver earrings.
The wind blows.
The wind was swirling and wild in the dark blue sky.
The sky is dark.
The sky is dark and gloomy, waiting for the sparkling lights of
                                      the moon and stars.

Kathleen Carroll (9)
St Gildas' RC Junior School

Sailing Boat By A Sea And Mountains

The trickling water flows angrily without faltering and never tires.
It tosses the tiny sailing boat like a rainbow lost in a storm.
The sandy beach, as yellow as the sun above, glistens as the tide
goes out,
Whilst the grass sways in the wind we cannot see.
The powerful waves punch against the rocks, preventing it from
escaping.
The messy cypress tree howls under the blue sky.

The mountains look beautiful from a distance,
But as you get closer, they crush you with ease.
They disguise everything behind them, they only let the dancing
sun peep through.
The candyfloss clouds drift slowly out into the sea-like sky.
The sun swirls like a Catherine wheel coughing off sparks into
the sky.

The deep blue sky jumps up high because of the heat of the hot sun.
The froth on the sea says 'hello' to its cousins, the clouds
And the shadow of the boat reaches out to its sister.
The multicoloured sail is the rainbow of the sea
And the wind blows the boat into its own world.

These all come together to make a world of happiness.

Roseanna Dundas (11)
St Gildas' RC Junior School

Starry Night

The lofty green tree is leaning over the sleepy village.
The silver moon is gleaming in the swirling night.
The glinting stars light up the midnight-blue sky.
The miniature houses have dazzling lights.
The lanky church is peaceful and towers over the quiet cottages.
The giant, emerald-green hills are sweeping and billowing
in the wind.

Jim Walker (9)
St Gildas' RC Junior School

The Winter's Night

It's a winter's night and I'm on the floor,
I can see a blue, shaded door.
It has raindrops wet and cold,
I see a light so shiny and bold,
If I went to school I would not have told.
For when I go inside, I have nowhere to hide,
Except I run to the field where you can pony ride.
I hear a bombshell,
Oh no, I fell.
I see a blur,
I don't know what to do.
My glasses have fallen off too and flown off in a zoom,
But just then I heard a boom!

Krystal Ude (8)
St Gildas' RC Junior School

Samuel's Zoo

In my bedroom I keep . . .
Ten rats that run about,
Nine bats that hang on the lamp,
Eight frogs who jump about,
Seven wolves who howl at night,
Six penguins in the wardrobe,
Five owls under the bed,
Four rhinos who knock the walls,
Three cats that sit around,
Two dogs who chase the cats,
And one . . . guess what?

Samuel Fernandez (8)
St Gildas' RC Junior School

Sailing Boat By A Sea And Mountains

The soft sand moves smoothly on the edge of the sea.
The cold, deep blue sea has many mysteries behind it, so beware.
It might look friendly, but don't judge by what you can see.
Oh please, please believe me my readers and remember,
                                        don't trust that sea!
The shaded, menacing, dangerous rocks are sharp and snappy
And also smooth, but can make fast moves!
The everlasting, long grass with many different colours,
Gets blown by the thunderous, pressurisng breeze.
Oh please don't trust that breeze!
And the boat, the wooden, colourful boat snores in the sun,
Its sail is bright as it smacks and spits at the wind.
The bright blue sky is staring at me
And the clouds are soft, foaming bits of milkshake as they lie
                                                    in Heaven.
The cypress tree attracts little creatures, insects and big,
                                                bulging bugs.
Oh sun, you're big and hot and bright,
You are out in the day, but not at night.
And finally, the beach - with laughing people enjoying themselves,
Oh, that could be me, me, me!

Louis Hennessey-Hicks (10)
St Gildas' RC Junior School

The Sunset

The sunset is so lovely
The sunset is so bright
I gaze at the many colours
As it's coming up to night.
It's way up in the sky
Up so very high
Reflecting off the sea
Staring back at me.

Mia Wolsey (8)
St Gildas' RC Junior School

What Is A Star?

What is a star?

A star is a daisy shining its little light onto Earth
So that mere passers-by can see its golden, miniature light.
The star is little pieces of silver glitter sprinkled all over the sky
To show travellers where to go.

Stars are like diamonds sparkling in the midnight black,
The stars shine into the midnight.
A star is gold, glistening in the sky,
Remember stars are white gold shining in the sky.

The star is a dandelion sprinkling its fluff all over the place,
It guides us through the night,
Shining its little light.

The star is a golden mystery.

Isobel Sinnott (9)
St Gildas' RC Junior School

My Aunty's Cupboard

In my aunty's cupboard she has many things.
She has . . .

Ten slippery ice creams that slip and slide
Nine flat plates that smash and clash
Eight clanking saucepans that clatter
Seven bendy forks and she puts them on the table
Six sharp knives that prick and will cut you
Five big spoons that you mix things with
Four strong spices that are really hot
Three big bowls that go with plates
Two crystal glasses that she drinks wine in
One teacup that she used to drink tea from.

Laurie Fitzgerald (8)
St Gildas' RC Junior School

Sailing Boat By A Sea And Mountains

The golden light shone in the sun's powerful gaze.
The waves pounded the rocks with the sound of a firing MP40.
The rocks have sharp edges which represent knives.
The grass is like a frantic rush for people to get to work.
The clouds in the sky look like fluffy candyfloss.
The sea looks like a mysterious place below ground.
The golden beach gets swallowed up when the tide comes in.
The rocks look like knives ready to attack the sea.
The sea keeps on having a merciless battle against itself.
The huge, looming mountains stand and watch the beach below.
The sun beams down like God's gaze watching the Earth below.
The sailing boat speeds across the vast, yet calm sea.
The waves run up the beach and back like a massive, frantic race.
The sky is like God's house floating in the blue sky,
God shines his sun down on the beach below.
The mountains are like a guardian watching the tiny beach like a
                                                                                hawk.
The tree is like a large lookout tower balanced badly on the
                                                                       ferociously high cliff.

Liam Bligh (10)
St Gildas' RC Junior School

A-J Of Today

A is for angel on top of my tree
B is for biscuit I dip in my tea
C is for candy all shiny and bright
D is for darkness, the opposite to light
E is for egg, I like them runny
F is for films that I think are funny
G is for girl, all pretty in pink
H is for Henry, all silly and old
I is for ice cream, all yummy and cold
J is for jelly, still in its mould.

Jessica Corrigan (8)
St Gildas' RC Junior School

Sailing Boat By A Sea And Mountains

The sun is shaped like a spiral in the sky, blinding our eyes.
The sun is coloured yellow like the light of the Lord.
The sun is like a ball in the sky, shining on us all.

The clouds are shaped like God's Heaven guiding our sun.
The clouds are coloured white like the angels watching us.
The clouds are like angels glittering around our eyes.

The mountains are shaped like triangles making triangle shadows.
The mountains are coloured purple to symbolise love.
The mountains are like the steps to God's remarkable home.

The sea smells like a royal perfume sent down from God.
The sea is coloured blue like the colour of peace.
The sea is like the rocky sounds of the springtime.

The grass is shaped like lines pointing up to God's lair.
The grass is coloured green like the watered grass.
The grass is like the hairs on a caterpillar pushing through.

The cypress trees are shaped like a Christmas tree.
The cypress trees are coloured green like a windy tree in Heaven.
The cypress trees are like a bunch of them in a rainforest in spring.

The sand smells like Jamaican rum sugar from the tropics.
The sand is coloured orange like the skin of an orange.
The sand is like a lift sending you to the kingdom of God.

I like the view because it's colourful
And it reminds me of the wonderful creations of God.

Tyrone Gaskin (10)
St Gildas' RC Junior School

What Is The Night?

The night is a black ghost across the sky,
Leaving a long trail of blood,
That is sometimes from little children lurking in the night.
Now it is midnight and he sees a little child
And now he knows it's his feast right now.

Danielle Sewell (9)
St Gildas' RC Junior School

What Is The Sea?

The sea is a blue dolphin
Splashing away.
It swims up and down
Crashing through.

The sea is a turquoise opal
Rippling round,
Making swift noises
Drifting around.

The sea is a bluey-green bag
Holding all the creatures
And coral inside,
Waiting to be opened.

The sea is a blob of blue ink
With ripples
Running everywhere.

The sea is an indigo whirlpool
Spinning
And sparkling away.

The sea is something
We have not yet explored!
Well, whatever the sea is
I like it in every way!

Holly Taylor (10)
St Gildas' RC Junior School

Untitled

Stars are tiny diamonds twinkling through the night.
Stars are glitter being sprinkled on a sheet of black paper.
Stars are fairy lights shining on a black wall.
Stars are opals gazing in outer space.
Stars are little candles guiding us through the night.
Stars are bulbs dazzling in the sky.
I love gazing at the dark, black night when stars look back at me.

Hayley Kimber (9)
St Gildas' RC Junior School

The Sea

The sea is a gigantic underwater empire
With a palace in the middle.

The sea is a blue and dazzling dolphin
Dancing in the sea.

The sea is a dolphin
Splashing its way to the horizon.

The sea is a dolphin
Making lots of wavy movements.

The sea is the most wonderful, magical
Place on Earth.

The sea is the most graceful
Place on Earth.

Daniel Sexton (9)
St Gildas' RC Junior School

The Sea

The sea is just a jumping dolphin, swimming towards the horizon.
In the sapphire-laden sea, a pod of whales swim along to feed.
The sea floor is like a magical kingdom with multicoloured coral
                                                for decoration.
The waves are like caressing ripples of jade moving to the beat
                                                of the wind.
The sea is just like a pinch of magic, the most amazing and
            mysterious thing on Earth, not yet fully explored.
The boats across the sea are like shiny, bobbing dots very far out
                                                in the water.
The streamlined creatures swimming in the water are just like
                        dark patches of fins and flippers.
The sea is the most magical, biggest, best kingdom on our planet.

Milena Messner (10)
St Gildas' RC Junior School

Sailing Boat By A Sea And Mountains

The boat sets sail on her mysterious journey,
The boat sets sail on her hunt for the cypress tree.
She sees a beach, hot and sandy,
She sees a mountain, cold and menacing.
Four rocks she sees, staring at her bow,
Four birds she sees, soaring in the vast sea-blue sky.
Towards the horizon dancing in the playful sun,
Towards an island, there is her goal.
Suddenly she sees it - look, a cypress tree,
Suddenly, see how many animals are near.
Her heart goes soft,
Her captain's too.
They leave the tree standing and smiling,
They leave the tree looking after others.
Off they go, stopping for a snack,
Off the island, leaving it be.
There they see their fine little town,
There they see their own homeland.
The clouds above them sing 'good day',
The trees next to them wave in the shade.
Up in the sky, Heaven is smiling,
Up there, up high.
To the town, they have been away for ten months,
To the men they have only been gone for ten days.

Hope Merritt (10)
St Gildas' RC Junior School

What Is Night?

The night is a gigantic damp box that opens at night,
Letting all its secrets out in the dark.
The night is like day, but in black
And it's very damp.
The night is a raven leaving a pile of deep footsteps
With a crow drifting through the sky.

Kevin Donkor (10)
St Gildas' RC Junior School

The Sea

The sea rolls like a rocking horse,
Thundering upon the beach.
The wave is like a giant hand
Crawling across the sand.

The blue, sparkling sea
Glitters in the sunshine.
The wind sighs
Over the ocean.

Aysha Starkey (9)
St Gildas' RC Junior School

What Is A Star?

What is a star?
A star is a bright light in the sky
Guiding your way home.
Its shine catches my eye
Right in the sky.
It's a planet,
It's a new world,
Waiting to be explored.

Mariella Lambrou (10)
St Gildas' RC Junior School

Sailing Boat By A Sea And Mountains

The soft sand being blown in one direction and then the other.
The ultraviolet sun burning all day long.
The grass whispering in the wind.
The mystic sea roaring and dancing.
The boat going into the menacing mountains, planning a landslide
                                              to ruin the fun.
The ragged rocks make a cosy docking bay.
The clouds waving and drifting in the kind, loving wind.
Last but not least, the caring tree loves all.

Henry Garcin (11)
St Gildas' RC Junior School

What Is A Star?

A star is a shining diamond dazzling in the night sky
Giving us light to see
And having its fun laughing and smiling
As if it was a golden key.

A star is a sparkling angel flying through the dark, thin air
Giving us golden love
But all people can see
Is a flashing spot above.

A star is a gift from Heaven looking over the dark, dim Earth
To help anybody that is at birth
The gift is there in town
Never letting us down.

Clare Walton (10)
St Gildas' RC Junior School

Footie Season

Vieira, Bergkamp and Henry,
Playing footie on the TV.
The Nigerian striker called Kanu,
Doing his skills in front of you.
All the supporters singing the song,
They continue all night long.
Roman Abramovic thinks he's rich,
All his cheap players keep on getting a stitch.
Nico Anelka sticks his hand in Ashley's face,
'Send him off, he's a disgrace!'
Real Madrid say they want Henry,
Arsenal say he's not for sale for any money.

Reiss Taylor (9)
St Gildas' RC Junior School

Sailing Boat By A Sea And Mountains

The sun is shaped like a golden beach ball floating in the sky
The sun is coloured bright like a shining torch in a dark room
The sun is like a flying copper coin in the bouncing out sky.

The clouds are shaped like squidgy sponges filled with foggy water
The clouds are coloured dullish, like dead suns put together
The clouds are like tiny particles of breath from an angry giant.

The mountains are shaped like pirate ships parked in the silent water
The mountains are coloured purple like the priest's robe at church
The mountains are like jagged blades of the sea.

The sea smells like fish, salt and filtered air
The sea is coloured crystal-blue like blue diamonds shining
 from the ground
The sea is like the handle that holds the blades.

The grass is shaped like waving spikes coming out of the ground
The grass is coloured green like leaves of a cypress tree
The grass is like the hairs of the world and the world is the head.

The cypress trees are shaped like green flames coming out of the
 blades
The cypress trees are coloured mixed green like the suit of a
 camouflaged soldier
The cypress trees are like a big fire put together.

The sand smells like wet, soggy salt
The sand is coloured gold like red, green and orange put together
The sand is like magic dust sprinkled on the ground.

I like the view because it is very relaxing and you can imagine
 yourself there.

Victor Lopez (10)
St Gildas' RC Junior School

Sailing Boat By A Sea And Mountains

The boat sails around like a shooting star
And the sail of the boat is like it is made out of the rainbow.

The sky smells like a blueberry pie,
It's sea-blue and crystal clear like a glittering diamond.

The sun is like a golden bow ready to be pulled.
It is beautiful and it shines like foil.
The sun bobs up and down like an excited baby getting a new toy.
It moves like a powerful falcon.

The clouds are like balls of wintry snow.
They are like ice cream with cream on top.
The clouds are calm and not like a wild dog on a lead
        jumping to get somewhere.

The waves are like a texture of royal-blue and sky-blue.
The waves grab onto the sand and then they let go.
The sand is golden yellow and it lies on the rocky, hard rocks.
The sand is like a builder's rough hands.
It almost smells like salty vanilla ice cream, delicious!

The grass waves in the bellowing, blowing wind.
It is like a lion's mane spread out.
The sea looks like a mysterious child hiding something.
The sea is smooth with a postponement to the bumpy waves.
It drifts away, away, away,
And then it is gone!

Shannon Greenaway (10)
St Gildas' RC Junior School

Sailing Boat By A Sea And Mountains

The multicoloured river walks slowly by,
The golden sand glows brightly in the sun,
White angels pass by in the sea-blue sky,
The singing wind says hello as he goes by.

The menacing mountains touch the sky,
Cypress tree (house of an elf) waves as the wind whooshes by.
The grass-green tickling hairs huddle up
And have a grass-green meeting.

The magical, glistening sun lights the Earth
Like a giant candle held up by God's hands.
The white, green and dark blue floss,
Slowly walks by as if it has been put into slow motion.

The multicoloured boat like a rainbow on the sea,
Floats calmly along the beautiful, boastful water.
The mast is like a fat stick,
Holding up the rainbow sail.

The ragged rocks coloured pink and purple,
Are as big as giant, coloured potatoes.

The multicoloured river walks slowly by,
The golden sand glows brightly in the sun,
White angels pass by in the sea-blue sky,
The singing wind says hello as he passes by.

Jazz Lyons-Foster (11)
St Gildas' RC Junior School

Sailing Boat By A Sea And Mountains

The sun is shaped like shining light from the colourful rainbow
The sun is coloured gold like a diamond sitting on a little cushion
The sun is like enjoying yourself with your friends.

The clouds are shaped like angels watching over us
The clouds are coloured white like snow falling on the floor
The clouds are like packets of snow dropping on your head.

The mountains are shaped like curved bridges
The mountains are coloured pink like heather flowers
The mountains are like lipgloss going on your lips.

The sea smells like slimy fish
The sea is coloured blue like the clouds
The sea is like starfish dancing in the sea.

The grass is shaped like curls falling from side to side
The grass is coloured green like a stem on a flower
The grass is like tickling flowers.

The cypress trees are shaped like flames going into the sky
The cypress trees are coloured green like the fields of London
The cypress trees are like volcanoes going up and down.

The sand smells like buzzing bees going in flowers
The sand is coloured gold like the statue of Queen Victoria
The sand is like the sun shining in the clouds.

I like the view because it is like the touch of God
And it feels like I'm there.
That is my view.

Katerina Makri (10)
St Gildas' RC Junior School

Sailing Boat By A Sea And Mountains

The sun is shaped like a wheel which is hypnotised
The sun is coloured yellow like an unrescued desert
The sun is like a strong beam that's hot as fire.

The clouds are shaped like Chinese prawn crackers
The clouds are coloured white like white, gleaming snowflakes
The clouds are like everlasting white flowers.

The mountains are shaped like lumpy hills
The mountains are coloured green like the evergreen leaves
The mountains are like paradise and a tropical island.

The sea smells like salt crystals gleaming here, there, everywhere
The sea is coloured blue like unrequited love
The sea is like angels swimming with their water wings.

The grass is shaped like baby weeds in the crystal clear sea
The grass is coloured light green like God and me were friends to be
The grass is like white polar bears sprinting with fear.

The cypress trees are shaped like the moon shining
The cypress trees are coloured green like my mum and dad
                                                    who I love
The cypress trees are like my imagination of a beach.

The sand smells like perfume and fresh air
The sand is coloured gold like me, because I'm golden-hearted
The sand is like a castle in my dream.

I like the view because it starts to blaze out
Through the wondrous sky
With God in my heart.

Hannah Adelowo (11)
St Gildas' RC Junior School

Sailing Boat By A Sea And Mountains

The sky is a sea of peace,
No storms will make it bad.
It can rampage like a rhino,
But it can always understand me.
The sky may have no ears,
But can always hear me.
From my first laugh to my last cry,
It will always be there.

The clouds are the beds for angels,
So long have I wished to touch them.
They are slow and soft,
The comfort me when I am down.
I love them so much,
The clouds may be big and slow,
But act as a brother to me,
I love them like a brother or sister.

The tall, menacing mountain towers above all,
It may look evil,
But inside it is as kind as spring.
Though the large giant sleeps and slumbers,
It will wake up when the last volcano has erupted
And will help all mankind.

The lush green cypress tree may look normal,
But it is the home of all fairies.
It is covered in leaves to hide itself from humans,
But it will always befriend me.
It grows like a child to an adult,
It is beautiful!

Joshua Morrison (10)
St Gildas' RC Junior School

Sailing Boat By A Sea And Mountains

As the boat glides across the sea,
The shining sun makes the boat
Smile like a little child.
The wavy clouds manoeuvre
Like a butterfly setting free.
The rough mountain stands
At the end of the cliff,
Showing off its beautiful colours.
When the cypress tree waves to the sun,
The sun makes the cypress tree sparkle
On its green, bright leaves.
The sandy beach twinkles
As the grass sways from side to side.

As the boat glides across the sea,
The cypress tree flickers,
Leaving droplets of rain behind.
The rocky mountains stand tall,
So all you can see are the colourful
Colours of the boat.
As the sea reflects all the beautiful colours,
The colours dance away
To shine in the orange and yellow sun.
The golden sand brings out the colour
Of the dark and light green grass.
The wavy grass in the golden sun
Shivers as the breeze blows it away.

Magita Baidoo (10)
St Gildas' RC Junior School

Winter Snow

Winter is so bright when covered with snow,
Soft like wool,
Fresh like water,
Smooth like skin on a newborn,
It glistens in the layer of snow carpet
Across the long fields.
Snow is tranquil,
Snow is beautiful when it's unblemished,
Snow is so magical, it catches your eyes.
Trees' branches turn from brown to white,
Children go out to play,
Snowmen and snowfights.
It's always such fun,
They don't notice the cold,
With scarves and gloves,
Hats and coats,
With the breeze in your face
Like an ice knife,
Careful, you might get frostbite.

Francesca Moglia (11)
St Martin of Porres RC Primary School

Lightning

Lightning is electric-blue, snow-white or red,
It's like a devil's fork, or a long piece of thread,
It feels the sky, but not stopping for a rest,
So if I were you, I would get out of bed.

Lightning brings a little breeze
And also brings a lot of fear,
It's very ferocious and brings a lot of tears,
People's homes and houses all get cleared.

Katie Foley (11)
St Martin of Porres RC Primary Schooll

Winter

Winter is like stars twinkling on the floor,
Or a bright diamond shining on a door,
The temperature of the snow is absolutely freezing,
So you may even start sneezing.

At your feet down below,
There is a lot of heavy snow,
It is a soft carpet of creamy white
And it is like porcelain in the night.

There are blocks of ice on your toes
And you can hardly move your frigid nose,
When you pick up the snow your teeth start to chatter
And when you drop the snow, it begins to scatter.

Johann Rajakarunanayake (11)
St Martin of Porres RC Primary School

Night sky

In the night, the sky turns crystal blue
Like my mum's peas,
When the fireworks are let off,
A nice row of vibrant and pretty colours appears,
Flashing and falling, spinning and crawling,
Oh, what a beautiful night this is.

Oh no, the stars are going, going, gone,
Yellow and orange, violet and ruby,
Can the sun be here already?
I must leave at once,
I must return home to my beautiful planet of red,
The red planet Mars,
I cannot wait till I tell my friends.

Winston Osei Tu-Tu (10)
St Martin of Porres RC Primary School

Winter Is Like . . .

Winter is a magical season,
I'm sure you'll agree,
Full of unblemished and deep snow.

The wind howls constantly,
Conjuring a light and airy breeze.
You feel like you have pinpricks
On your freezing cold face!

You look up and see a dull, pale sky,
With the sun popping out behind the trees.

The snow is like a powdery road,
Leading to fun and excitement,
But the clouds just sit in the sky,
Looking like blotches of wool.

Winter is a magical season,
I'm sure you'll agree,
Full of unblemished and deep snow.

Laura Piccirillo (10)
St Martin of Porres RC Primary School

Lightning!

Lightning is ferocious,
Dusty-grey and light pink.
It's full of menace and devil's blood
And rather strong and fierce.
If you get hit by lightning,
You will get an electric shock,
It will hurt very much,
So stay away and just look!

Lauren Malone (11)
St Martin of Porres RC Primary School

Shooting Stars

Shooting stars cluster together,
Travelling in any weather.
Any colour, red, yellow or blue,
Or even white like glue.

Shooting stars, swirly like an 'S',
When you look at pictures, they're rather like a mess!
Big ones, small ones, look around,
Beautiful and pretty,
Spiral like a spring.

One night I thought, *bring me up to the sky,
I want to see what you feel like - jelly, hot or fluid*?
But then again, I'll stick to the ground,
Just in case you're horrid.

Erin Farrell (10)
St Martin of Porres RC Primary School

Winter

Winter, winter all around,
The birds are singing
As the sun is dying.
Some light, clear crystals
Started gliding down from above.
As the howling wind screeches softly
And once again in the wintry month,
The snow must melt and as it does,
So the fun disappears and the snow turns to slush.

Amira Gharbi (11)
St Martin of Porres RC Primary School

Dream Of Winter

Winter snow falls like rice in a pan,
It lies heavy on the roofs of houses,
On grass, ground, everywhere is full.
It's like paper, a carpet of snow,
It's fun to play in, it's better than rain,
It comes with clouds and a beautiful sky.
When you walk in fresh snow, it makes a crunching sound,
Fresh snow, fresh snow is magical.
Snow, snow, falling from above, heavy and light.
It falls like a sheet of snow.
In a blizzard it's like a bunch of snow eagles swishing around.
Snowballs flying everywhere,
I love the snow better than the rain, remember that.

Luke Mead (10)
St Martin of Porres RC Primary School

The Night Sky

The night sky is lovely,
When all the stars are out,
It's a wonderful sight,
The stars are shimmering,
The moon is glistening in the sky,
It stays like that till the morning,
When the sun comes out
And loses its shimmer and glisten,
The lovely sky will come again tonight.

Hannah McKirdy (10)
St Martin of Porres RC Primary School

Winter Wonderland

The scene is turning white
While the snow piles up.
Making snowmen, building igloos
Drinking cocoa cups.

Dazzling white diamonds
Are enriching the skies,
Melting leisurely as they fall
And waiting to eventually die.

As in Caribbean islands
Or near the Mediterranean Sea,
While camels roam the desert sands
We'll be walking in a winter wonderland!

Alessandro Fontanini (11)
St Martin of Porres RC Primary School

The Night Sky

I'm sitting here alone under the pitch-black sky
But silly me, how could it be?
I'm not alone, the sky's with me.

Fiery red, crystal blue are my favourite colours too,
There's loads more fun to be found,
Just lying on this old, wet ground.

The stars all shining down at me,
Laughing and joking,
How could it be?

Elle Rolph (10)
St Martin of Porres RC Primary School

Ferocious Storm

Electric blue's sizzling around me,
I look at the sea!
Whooshing waves, millions of metres high!
Booom!
It's laughing, a cackling
Witch's laugh.

It's like the centre of a leaf's vein, dripping!
Washing me like a shower!
It's scampering along, going so fast,
Nothing can keep up!

It's fizzing, like a sherbet drink,
It won't, it can't stop!
There's orange smoke,
It's like a firework display,
Showing off every second!

If there was anything beautiful,
Like flowers, or trees and all before,
They are all singed,
It's furious!
It's mad!
Exotic colours swimming,
Like a moving painting!

It's making lakes, I'm sure the river will overflow!
It's as though it will never stop!

Louise Parsons (10)
St Martin of Porres RC Primary School

The Midnight Mystery

I'm all alone,
On this dark, dark night.
I see shadows everywhere I roam.
I see a flash of lightning,
It looks so much like a camera flash,
Then a loud *boom!*
I jump out of my skin,
I search for my bright moon,
But I have to fend for myself.
I see mixed colours,
Electric-blue, mighty green and clashing red,
But still I fight the storm.
My eyes are glazed with fear,
As I hear the rumbling sound.
I am frozen to the solid ground,
The falling rain hits me
Like a slap in the face.
Then suddenly I hear a crash,
Yet I still stand my ground.
Luminous shapes come towards me,
But who?
And why?
I don't understand.
I dodge the lightning
And I fall to the ground . . .

Ania Shannon (11)
St Martin of Porres RC Primary School

The Storm

The devastating storm fills the sky with sparks.
Luminous red flashes appear in my vision as I back away rapidly.
Crackle! Crash! Boom!
The midnight sky floods with forks of fluorescent lightning.
As drums beat in my ears, I feel as if I am stabbed.
Children's mouths are open wide
As they stare at the tree branches reaching to grab them.
Whoosh! The destructive flash of light moves away to bother
                                          someone else.

Anya Fitzpatrick (10)
St Martin of Porres RC Primary School

Butterfly

Butterfly, oh butterfly, your colour is so nice,
Your wings are made of white and blue, just like coloured ice.
When I look at you, you remind me of the rainbow,
Flying high in the sky as your wings glide to and fro.
I will see you another day, bye-bye beautiful butterfly.

Simi Solebo (9)
St Martin's Prep School

Sunshine

S is for the sun glancing down at me
U is for umbrella that I use on rainy days
N is for nasty weather like a twirling tornado
S is for storm that whips up the wind
H is for hurling lightning like arrows from the sky
I is for icicles thrusting towards the earth
N is for nice weather with a clear blue sky
E is for English weather that always surprises you.

Alexander Glassman (9)
St Martin's Prep School

The Snow

Snow is so amazingly white,
It makes a wonderful, colourful sight.
It started on the day before yesterday,
I woke up and saw soft, slushy snow.
I got some clothes on and went into the garden,
It was cold as a winter's day.

After a while I built a snowman,
Then I began to cheerfully play.
After a while the snowman began to say,
'Go back in! Go back in!'
So I went back in and began to pray.
In under an hour I thought of snow
And the direction in which it could blow.

Zachariah Johnson (9)
St Martin's Prep School

February Is My Birthday

The trees are starting to bloom
And it's my birthday very, very soon.
The birds are singing in the trees,
While I am sitting in the breeze.
My mum told me to come inside,
Because it was time for my birthday surprise.
Lots of people in the house,
Including James, my pet mouse.
Now it's time for my chocolate delight,
I am going to eat it with all my might.
All my presents sporty like,
Fantastic, just what I like.
The days are short and cold,
But I am happy because I am another year old.

Brodie Berman (9)
St Martin's Prep School

Bedtime

Bedtime is the end of a day
When the sun goes down
And the moon comes up
All the children get into bed
And lay down their sleepy head
Some of the children dream
And some snore
The tape recorder goes off
And they wake up with a fright
They go back to sleep
And sleep deep all night
The morning awaits the sleepy children
And the moon goes down
And the sun comes up.

Louie King (8)
St Martin's Prep School

As I Walk

As I walk through the dewy grass,
My unshod feet making no sound,
I see little shoots, that until now,
Have been hiding underground.

As I walk through the dewy grass,
I see rosebuds, readying themselves to bloom.
I can just imagine a single rose,
Under the crescent moon.

As I walk through the garden of spring,
A smile plays around my face,
For now, on an early March morning,
There is no lovelier place.

Kayla Marks (10)
St Martin's Prep School

My Family

Mum, Mum, get off the phone
I am bored, I am playing alone.
Zach, Zach, give me the photos back
Don't take anything out of my rucksack.
Grandad, Grandad, have you lost your teeth?
Who could it be? I think a thief.
Grandma, Grandma, get out your sewing kit
And make me a jumper that will fit.
Dad, Dad, your bills are here
And there is nothing to fear.
Jenny, Jenny, turn the music down
Why don't you go shopping in town?
Now you know all about my family
And they are all a part of me.

Erin-Louise Adams (8)
St Martin's Prep School

The Great White Shark

Gliding through the murky waters with its fearsome jaws,
Camouflaging itself from its prey at the bottom of the sea
And then launching itself like a rocket,
It rips its prey's flesh into compact pieces.
Scavenging prey from others' successful kills,
Its rough, scaly skin is like a rag,
This predator is one of the best in the whole wide world.

Sina Sharifi (10)
St Martin's Prep School

Mum

Our mum called Elain has a brain like a sieve,
She forgets where the things in her kitchen all live,
Like there will be milk in the cupboard,
And plates in the fridge,
That's our mum Elain with a brain like a sieve.

Ria Chitroda & Amber Patel (9)
St Martin's Prep School

My Busy Birthday

I got out of bed at ten to seven,
I looked at my presents and thought, *what heaven.*

I ate an apple on a chair,
Then ate my breakfast over there.

I opened two presents, some with a card,
What's that noise? The dustmen in the yard.

I got myself dressed and ready for school
And got my swimming kit ready for Park Road pool.

Down the road and in through the gate,
I thought I might have been, but I wasn't late.

Maths, maths, assembly, play,
Literacy, lunch and that's half a day.

The class went swimming and nobody drowned,
So it's back to school and sweets all round.

To the music centre for the intermediate strings,
Where I learn how to play all sorts of things
(on my violin).

To Pizza Express for my birthday tea,
With my mum, brother, dad and . . . *me!*

Tom Andrews (10)
Weston Park Primary School

Planets

I couldn't believe my luck
I was sharing my tuck
With the man on the moon
Who was holding a balloon
Green cheese and cucumber rolled into a sandwich
Looked gross
But tasted quite nice
But it could have done with a bit of rice.

I decided to leave him and visit Earth
After all it was the place of my birth
Earth is nice
Except for mice
Oh and the ice
But as you know, holidays can't last
I had to leave very fast!

Next I went to Mars
And ate a couple of bars
You see it helps me grow
A couple of enormous toes!
Mars is red but quite cold
Watch out! You've been told
Mars is nice
If you're a block of ice.

Now do you want to leave and have an adventure
Or
Do you want to stay and fix a denture?

Shanti Chahal (9)
Weston Park Primary School

Haiku Trouble

I am sad because
I can't think of a haiku
Here in the classroom.

Ayla Richardson (11)
Weston Park Primary School

My School

I like my school
Because it's so cool.
We may not have a pool
But we get to play football.
We all play in the sun
We all have lots of fun.
Sarah is our teacher
Sometimes she is a preacher
But she is a good teacher.
Mr Wickham is our headmaster
He makes us work even harder.
We are always doing work
Tuesdays we get our homework.
Our school is called Weston Park
And it is right next to a park
And will always be my school.

Dhru Patel (8)
Weston Park Primary School

My Lovely Dad, Ted

My dad, Ted
Likes to lie in bed.
When he does
He's such a sleepyhead.
He is big and strong and tall
He is the biggest of us all.
Dad likes to watch football matches
And he shouts when a goal he catches.
Arsenal is his favourite team
Man United makes him scream.
When he's away, he calls on the phone
He doesn't like being alone.
I love my dad
And feel sorry for him when he's sad.

Nina Rose Law Keen (7)
Weston Park Primary School

I'm One Big Animal Family

I'm as lively as a leopard
'Cause I'm on the loose
I run around with all my might
You can't catch me.

I'm cheeky like a monkey
Swinging in the trees
I'm full of fun and lots of laughs
You can't catch me.

I gulp like a goldfish
In the deep blue sea
I don't care if a shark comes by
'Cause he can't catch me.

I'm as sneaky as a little mouse
Munching all the food
And when the big fat ginger cat comes
He can't catch me.

I'm a snuggly teddy bear
You can cuddle up to me
I'm full of love and happiness
You can catch me.

Lily Biglari (8)
Weston Park Primary School

Monday's Child (2004 Edition)
(Based on 'Monday's Child')

Monday's child is filled with junk
Tuesday's child is full of funk
Wednesday's child loves watching TV
Thursday's child can hardly see
Friday's child loves maths and school
Saturday's child is extra cool
But the child that is born on the coolest day
Is like no other and loves to play.

Gwithyen Strongman (11)
Weston Park Primary School

Me!

I'm as funny as a monkey
And I love drawing.
I'm really quite funky
And when I'm hungry,
My tummy starts roaring.

I love to climb trees,
I'm as tall as a sunflower,
I can jump very high,
While bending my knees.
I get a shiver down my spine,
When I taste lemons
That are sour.

Now you've heard
Nearly all about me,
My tummy's roaring,
So it must be time for tea!

Madeleine Sellers (7)
Weston Park Primary School

Ellen

My sister Ellen
I asked if she'd like some melon
Of course the answer was yes
She always makes a mess.
Every day and morning
She is always yawning.
She really likes dogs
She doesn't mind frogs.
She really likes French
She never sits on a bench.
Uh-oh! Here's Ellen eating melon!

Owen Gillespie (7)
Weston Park Primary School

Skater Rock

Skater rock it's the best thing,
Skater rock, hear the skaters sing.

Skater rock, it's everywhere,
Skater rock, it's smashing thin air.

Skater rock, it's getting mad,
Skater rock, it's more than bad.

Skater rock, break the rules,
Skater rock, it's not for fools.

Skater rock, it's one big crime,
Skater rock, it's a matter of time.

Skater rock, it's only for dudes,
Skater rock, get in the mood.

Louis Abbott Wilson (9)
Weston Park Primary School

My Cousin, Kayah

My baby cousin, Kayah, was born on Christmas Day,
I've taught her how to clap her hands
And copy words I say.

Now she's 13 months,
She likes fish fingers and chips for lunch,
Munch, munch, munch.

I love my Kayah to bits,
Just like a big banana split.

Shyanne Duffus (8)
Weston Park Primary School

The Knight And The Fairy Queen

'Oh, what is wrong mighty knight?
You, who are usually in flight,
To fight the foe and find the grail,
Why, oh why do you cry and fail?'

'I went to see the Fairy Queen,
Who is the most beautiful creature ever seen,
But something terrible happened to me,
So awful, it felt like I was stung by 1,000 bees!'

'So what happened, oh mighty one?
What evil thing was done?'

'The first time I saw her it was at a glance,
My love for her was so strong, I was in a trance.
But as soon as I got near to the Fairy Queen,
My love was over, so it seemed.

For she had turned quite ugly and began to cackle,
Her skin all mouldy had started to crackle.
I turned to run and run and run,
But stopped because the evil was not yet undone.

I couldn't remember my name, my home,
I couldn't remember even why I roamed!'

'I am so sorry, brave knight,
Can you remember how to fight?'

'Alas, I cannot, I have failed this world,
My pride is gone and my joy has furled.
So now I will venture on,
Until my life has gone.'

Lily Bradley (10)
Weston Park Primary School

My Visit To The Beach

When we arrived the sky was blue
And the sea was very dark
My brother was worried he'd get eaten by a shark.
My sister and I had a race
When I won
She went red in the face.
She started shouting at me
So I went swimming in the sea.
She threw her shoe at my head
I said, 'That's enough'
And kicked her instead.
So *she* told Mum
Mum went mad
And told us off for being bad.
We missed out on all the treats
Including ice cream flavoured sweets.
We went to explore the caves
Across the tide and through the waves.
My brother found a crab
My sister found a leech
And we all fed it peach.
On the way home
I saw a terrible sight
My brother and sister had a fight.
She poked him in the eye
He called her a custard pie.
After a while I fell asleep
And dreamed of dancing sheep.

Lucinda Hetherington (10)
Weston Park Primary School

The Poem Competition

I was trying to write a poem.
Then I thought of it,
I said to myself, 'I'll show 'em!'

I'll beat 'em all,
They don't stand a chance
And when I beat them,
They'll all start to bawl.

This morning I'm going to school,
We will read our poems today.
Before we read our poems,
We have to swim in the pool.

Here come the marks,
I bet I'll get 10/10.
5/10! 'I couldn't read your writing
And it looks like you've been drawing sharks'.

Kairan Howard-Shawbell (9)
Weston Park Primary School

Tae Kwon Do

Before I start the class of Tae Kwon Do
I adjust my belt and kimono
We bow and stand in a line
Our instructor tells us to do our warm-ups
We run, jump, do press-ups and sit-ups
We're out of breath and want a rest
But he says no, straight to our patterns test
We block, punch, chop and kick
We're tired out and sweaty, that's the trick
Our instructor tells us to form a circle and bow
All together we shout, *1, 2, 3 Tae Kwon Do*
It is the end now
It is time to go!

André Caudebec (9)
Weston Park Primary School

20th Century War

Like cannons rolling through the night
unmistakably asking for a fight
all they want is more, more, more,
stuck in a 20th century war.

Swords are swishing,
boulders rolling,
as if someone is going bowling,
all they want is more, more, more,
stuck in a 20th century war.

Planes are bombing,
ear donging, boom and bang, away they go,
all they want is more, more, more,
stuck in a 20th century war.

All they want is more, more, more,
stuck in a 20th century war,
boom and *bang* and *bong!*

Boo Jackson (9)
Weston Park Primary School

Surfing At Bondi Beach

On New Year's Day down in Sydney, Australia,
Surfing at Bondi Beach, I wouldn't be a failure.
The sun was shining up in the sky,
As I got on my bodyboard and waved the beach goodbye.
The waves were very big, acting like a slide,
On my super bodyboard I was riding the tide.
But sometimes the currents were catching me in a rip,
So I did a flip like a sinking ship.
The waves were speeding me onto the sand,
I felt like I was still surfing, but I was on land.
When I got out two hours later,
I said to the surf, 'See you later alligator.'

Luke Rowan (10)
Weston Park Primary School

Rudolph's Holiday

For my holiday I'm stuck,
Riding on a pick-up truck.

I'm going to a reindeer enclosure,
I've heard there's lots of sun exposure!

So I decide to pack,
Three bottles of suncream and my sun hat,
No more carrying Santa's sack!

But when I get there, what do I see?
No jam scones, no cream tea!

I'm used to class!
A crystal bowl, not glass!

Santa Claus take me back!
I'll carry your smelly sack!

Anything is better than staying in this dirty hole!
I'd rather get a lump of coal!

Santa Claus take me today!
I really didn't want to go anyway!

I'm sure you like me under all that fat
And that *really* stupid hat!

Sorcha Bradley (10)
Weston Park Primary School

If I Was A Cat

If I was a cat, I'd stay out all night,
If I was a cat, I'd have parties 'til light.

If I was a cat, I'd climb everywhere,
If I was a cat, I'd chase every hare.

If I was a cat, I'd have fun all day,
If I was a cat, I'd jump and play.

If I was a cat and you were a mouse,
I'd chase you all day around the house.

Evie Lewis (9)
Weston Park Primary School

Flea-Man

A man with a boot
Had to shoot
The ball into the net
He's a lean, mean, killing machine
And hasn't missed one yet.

The ball ploughed
Into the crowd
The player fell to his knees
He started to itch
And ran round the pitch
It turned out he had fleas.

A little old man
With a frying pan
Hit the ball right back
The goalie took a kick
He hit it rather quick
It landed with a mighty whack.

Flea-man attacked
The ball with a smack
It went zooming into the net.
Those fleas made him mad
And he turned really bad
He'll get a hat-trick I bet.

Karl Packham (9)
Weston Park Primary School

Winter

W is for windy weather
I is for the icy ground
N is for neat and tidy snow, until children play in it
T is for tiny flakes of snow falling from the sky
E is for empty trees without foliage
R is for roofs that are covered in snow.

Emma Jimdar (8)
Weston Park Primary School

Missing You, Bear

Have you ever wondered where lost bears go to play?
Well, here's a little story to brighten up your day.

It's about my little bear who was left upon a train,
And how joy became sadness - how sunshine turned to rain.

I didn't see him drop underneath my seat,
For I was too busy eating my sweet!

By the time I noticed my precious toy's fate,
The train had pulled away and it was too late!

My days were filled with sadness and despair,
My bedtimes were like a living nightmare.

Mum and Dad tried their best to make me feel better,
But they couldn't put my heart back together.

Nearly two years later, the doorbell rang at dawn,
The postman had appeared - I was too shocked to yawn!

When I opened the package, what did I see?
Little bear - yes, he was there - he had come back to me.

Scott Cadman (9)
Weston Park Primary School

The Lonely Dragon

There once was a dragon all lonely and sad,
He lived in a cave with no mum or dad.
He sobbed in his cave because no one came near,
When he breathed fire he filled the people with fear.

One night a little girl heard the dragon cry
She wondered if he was going to die.
She slowly walked by and went into his lair,
She heard him wailing that nobody cared.
She said, 'It's OK, I'll be your friend,'
And everyone loved him in the end.

Aisling Reidy Martin (9)
Weston Park Primary School

A Pair Of Tap Shoes

Once upon a time there were a pair of tap shoes
Waiting to be bought.
They were in the shop window longing to be useful.
They were sparkly gold
Waiting to be sold.

But one day a little girl came along and . . .
Bought me!
She said, 'I want them because they are
All pretty and glittering and new and
I think they would be the perfect shoe.'

The tap show was brilliant
My flap was just right
My ball-change was sweet
And my drop was exactly on the beat.

But now showtime is over
And I am alone and forgotten
Returned to my box
And replaced with new black tap shoes
I shudder with fear
I guess I will have to wait 'til next year.

Megan Jones (9)
Weston Park Primary School

Playtime

I like it at school
I think it is cool.

Playtime is best
Better than the rest.

You can run about
Scream and shout.

It's always over too soon
Got to go back to the classroom.

Eleni Odyssea Barnett (8)
Weston Park Primary School

My Hallowe'en

Today is Hallowe'en
I saw a black dog
What does that mean?

Travellers beware
Black dogs mean death
Everywhere!

Witches in the air
On their brooms
Everywhere!

Vampires having a bite
On people's necks
What a sight!

Dr Frankenstein making his creation
Walking around
All of the nation

Zombies with no brains
Walking around
Showing their veins

Werewolves wailing at night
Changing their form
Having a fight.

Callum Midson
Weston Park Primary School

My Dad, Nader

My dad, Nader
He used to be a farmer
With long black hair
And milk to share
Well I must say, he liked to be fair
But he's still called Nader
And he's still my father!

Laura Mokhtari (7)
Weston Park Primary School

Food

Banana splits
With apple pips,
Juicy pears
With chocolate stairs.
Chocolate bars
And fruity cars,
Apple rings
And liquorice strings.
Cheesy dippers
And lots of kippers,
Lollipops
And lots of crops.
Food
Food
Is the
Best.

Ellie Whitlock (7)
Weston Park Primary School

Alien Zigzag

Alien Zigzag is a very strange alien,
His face is totally blue and green,
He has one large eye in the centre of his face,
With a mouth that is curvy and mean.

He attacks all he sees,
As he flies around space,
From his fingers come lasers,
Aimed at the face.

Joanna Clarke (8)
Weston Park Primary School

Tennis Ball

I spin, I swerve,
I whizz, I curve.

I go so fast, I go so slow,
So watch me go.

Hit, whack,
There and back.

Into the net,
That's a let.

In, out,
The linesmen shout.

High as the trees,
New balls please!

Joe Moody (9)
Weston Park Primary School

Books

Books, books are so cool,
Horrid Henry is a fool,
I am reading 'Lion Boy'
And I'm having real joy.

There are lots of different types,
There are even books on bikes.
Books with pictures,
Books with words,
Books with dolphins,
Books with birds.

Books to borrow,
Books to buy,
Books to make you laugh
And cry.

Jack Tully (9)
Weston Park Primary School

The Loch Ness Monster

Deep within Loch Ness,
There is a scary monster,
Mightier than the lioness,
Its gnashing teeth will crush you to bits.

It eats every scrap,
In its path,
It is totally a human trap,
It will strip your flesh to bones.

It swiftly swoops around the lake,
Searching for prey in its way,
It does not need friends or a mate,
It just needs supper.

Elizabeth Norton (8)
Weston Park Primary School

Seasons

This is the season that most people like,
When the cherries grow and the apples alike,
And the plants and trees grow so tall,
And the sun in the clear sky, the sun like a ball,
And the flowers bloom, marigolds and all,
And the curling ivy climbs up the brick wall.

This is the season that trees dislike,
When the white snow falls on icy spikes,
And bare trees wither and all is not well,
And the frozen snow, ten inches it fell,
And the freezing ice is under a spell,
And the cold numbs your skin and you shall yell.

Jian Chiang Poh (9)
Weston Park Primary School

My Hamster, Muffin

Muffin likes to sleep,
Muffin can drive my toy Jeep,
Muffin likes to eat,
And when he does, he's very sweet.

Muffin can do the monkey bars,
He can jump so high, he can touch the stars.
Muffin's ever so fat,
He's bigger than his paper mat.

He spins on his wheel,
The speed he can feel,
Then he has a quick drink,
That helps him to think.

When he lies on his bed,
He cuddles his ted,
Then without a doubt,
He's up and about.

I like him best when he climbs
On my arm,
That's when I know,
He won't come to any harm.

He's one in a million,
He's just the best,
He's the only one for me,
I don't need the rest.

Adrienne Webster (8)
Weston Park Primary School

My Family

I have a big brother called Dom
Who is always singing a song
His voice is so manky
It makes us all cranky
We need earplugs all day long.

Saffron Lashley (10)
Weston Park Primary School

Skateboarding Heaven

Ollie
Darkslide
Varial kickflip.

Melon
Indy
Airwalk
Heelflip.

180° ollie spinning around
Grinding on a grinding pole
Nailed to the ground.

Skating up a vert ramp
I'm flying through the air
Tailslide
Boardslide
I don't really care.

Good trucks
Great deck
Grip tape really fine
Ready to rock
Ready to roll
Because skateboarding's
Not
A
Crime!

Rufus Crewe-Henry (8)
Weston Park Primary School

My Blanket

My blanket is special to me
Because I had it since I was a baby.
Whether it is in shreds or whether it's neat
Whether it smells like a piece of meat
I will love it more and more
Until I'm knocking at your door.

Millie Page (8)
Weston Park Primary School

The Racing Horse

Brownie was a horse who belonged to a man,
The horse loved to run of course, the man's name was Fran.

Until one day he was in the mail
Quicker than a snail,
For he'd been put in the Ebay sale.

For Fran couldn't keep up the rent
And didn't want to live in a tent.

Soon he was at the gate of his new mate,
His mate was a jockey who preferred to play hockey.

The next day,
Before he could say neigh,
He was at the race track,
Brownie thought, *what muck,*
For there didn't seem much luck.

The day after that,
He was in the race
At a terrific pace.

He was in every race and won them all
And his jockey gave up hockey.
Until one day he lost the race,
'Not 1st,' his jockey cried, 'not 2nd, not 3rd,
But last.
You were not at all fast.'

Now he's been put away,
They say in the stable,
For he had got old and was sold.

Ellen Gillespie (9)
Weston Park Primary School

Heartbreak

A strike of lightning in your heart
A fragment of glass falls from your eye
A blazing fire in your throat
A black cloud forming in the sky.

He looks at you
You turn away
You remember when
You used to play.

You close your mind
Try to forget
Everything that's around
But still you hear the beating sound.

You run away
And try to hide
And you think about
The time you cried.

Then you stand up and say
'I'm not afraid of him
Why should I stand here
And let him win?'

So you run to the crowd and shout aloud
'I'm not scared anymore, I'm going to talk to him'
So you turn around
And walk off with a grin.

Romany Crewe-Henry (11)
Weston Park Primary School

Barbados

Barbados, you are so sunny
And I'll come over
I'll spend all my money

Barbados, Barbados, come and play
I can't resist to
Come every day

Barbados, Barbados, I'll ring you tonight
I'll come over
On the morning flight

Barbados, Barbados, I'll see you tomorrow
I don't want to leave
But I'll go back in sorrow.

Jamilla Walcott (9)
Weston Park Primary School

People

People good
People bad
People really, really sad
People fat
People thin
People with a hairy chin
People white
People black
People with a bony back
People old
And people bold.

Kamilah Jogee (7)
Weston Park Primary School

Where Is The Moon?

Where is the moon?
The moon is in the sky but can't be seen at noon.
Where is Mars?
Mars is our red planet but I hope it has some bars.
Where is Saturn?
Saturn is four planets away with its rings shining all day.
Where is Pluto?
Pluto is way, way, far away!
Where is our Milky Way?
The Milky Way is up, up high, reaching across the night-time sky.
Where are we?
We are on Earth, the only place where there is life.
Where is the sun?
The sun is very, very bright, brings us all that light.

Helin Sertkaya (9)
Weston Park Primary School

Goodnight

The stars are twinkling,
I'm not blinking,
My mouth is open,
My eyes are shut,
My mum's downstairs,
I'm in bed,
Dreaming of things,
I have in my head.

Zulaikha Bedwei-Majdoub (10)
Weston Park Primary School

Modern City

A city is more than you think,
Retailers, second-hands,
But remember, there aren't any
Rock bands!

Shops here, shops there,
Shops *everywhere!*
Selling this, selling that,
Everything in them,
Including a *cricket bat!*

So you see,
Don't be witty
And join the
Modern city!

Deniz Genc (8)
Weston Park Primary School

Snow

Snow, snow, beautiful snow,
Snow, snow, wonderful snow,
All glistening and white
And very, very bright.

Snow, snow, lovely snow,
All soft like ice cream.

Snow, snow, you are the best,
You make me happy,
Like a baby in a dry nappy.

Daisy Webb (9)
Weston Park Primary School

My Bed

I love my bed
Because I can relax my head.
I can sleep all the time
And I can think of a rhyme.
I can have a dream
And with a beam.
I can sleepwalk
And I can talk.
I can think in my bed
And I can blink with my ted.
When I am awake
I can think of something to make.
I just love my bed.

Jay-Ann Harriott (8)
Weston Park Primary School

Pooey Louis

My brother Louis smells of pooey,
He has scruffy hair and big brown eyes,
Just like a bear.
He's a messy little so and so
And I should know.
He screams, shouts and runs about,
But I don't care.
He's my pooey Louis little brother,
With big brown eyes
Just like a bear.

Stephanie Saunders (8)
Weston Park Primary School

Snow

Snow, covering the world in a thick, white blanket
Snow, watching it fall lightly from where I sit
Snow, like sparkling crystals falling down
Snow, falling from the sky on my head like a diamond crown
Snow, shouting, run, a red nose
Snow, freezing cold from our heads to our toes.

Bianca Kessna-Irish (11)
Weston Park Primary School

Football

F is for fun, football is fun.
O is for the opportunity we have to play football.
O is for open, the goal is open.
T is for trainers, we play football in trainers.
B is for ball, we play football with a ball.
A is for attack, we attack players in football.
L is for look, we look for players.
L is for learning, we like to learn how to play football.

David Costa (10)
Wyvil Primary School

Beautiful Butterfly

B is for beautiful, butterflies are very beautiful.
E is for exciting, they are very exciting.
A is for angels, butterflies are like angels up above.
U is for up, they fly up everywhere.
T is for talent, they have great talent.
I is for intelligent, butterflies are extremely intelligent.
F is for form, butterflies are formed perfectly.
U is for unique, all butterflies are very unique.
L is for lovely, butterflies are so lovely.

Rebekah Foster (9)
Wyvil Primary School

The Wind

When the wind is howling between the trees,
It is a wolf searching for its lost cubs.

When the wind is wild,
It is a T-rex attacking anything.

When the wind is mad,
It is a rhinoceros attacking anything.

When the wind is calm,
It is a baby fast asleep.

When the wind is crazy,
It is a robot out of control.

When the wind is really, really cold,
It is like the North Pole.

When the wind is really, really strong,
People and animals fly.

When the wind is really, really quiet and really, really calm,
You can barely hear a sound,
Not even the sound of the sea or the rattle of the trees.

Zakwan Awangkechik (10)
Wyvil Primary School

Hip Hop

I'm hip, I'm hop
I'm doing the bop
Do you know what?
I'm thinking of that dog, he bites
But I don't fight because my message is
Love.

Ti yanne Pemberton-Wright (8)
Wyvil Primary School

Wind And Sea

When the wind is howling between the buildings,
It is a wolf desperately searching for its lost cubs.

When the wind is whispering through the trees,
It is calling out sweet melodies.

All you can hear are leaves blowing in the air.

The shore slashes from side to side,
And you won't believe your eyes.

When doves fly around the sea,
It brings peace to you and me.

The sea is just light and clear,
It slithers round like a snake that doesn't care.

I love the sea very much,
It gives me a gentle touch.

Sasha Ferdinand (9)
Wyvil Primary School

Windy Days

When the wind is howling between the buildings,
It is a wolf killing its prey.
When the wind is breaking the branches,
It is a monkey jumping free.
When the wind is whispering between the trees,
It is a bumblebee searching for its honey.
When the wind is sharp and brisk,
It is a bird pecking all the leaves on the tree.
When the wind is scattering leaves,
It is an ant fighting for food.
When the wind is blowing umbrellas inside out,
It is a lion in a bad mood.

Jaylee Ali (10)
Wyvil Primary School

The Queen's Word

The Queen's word
Is such a bird
She climbed on top
But nearly dropped
She rang the bell
But then she fell
I wonder why
She cannot fly?

The Queen's word
Is such a bird
But on and on she goes
She went to bed
Then bumped her head
So she lay down for a doze.

Abigail Ashmead (8)
Wyvil Primary School

Helen Keller

H is for Helen for that was her name,
E is for excellent, her learning was excellent,
L is for learning, she loved to learn,
E is for exciting, she lived a very exciting life,
N is for noble, she was very noble.

K is for Keller for that was her surname,
E is for explore, she liked to explore,
L is for lonely, she was never lonely,
L is for lovely, flowers are lovely,
E is for education, she had a good education,
R is for responsible, everyone is responsible.
   I love Helen Keller.

Sarah Osei-Owusu (10)
Wyvil Primary School

The Lady Of The Countryside

There, her eyes twinkle in the night
Though . . . who sees her eyes brightly white?
But maybe she is as shy as a mouse
So how can she cope staying in the Weatherfield house?

Turn around and see the girl
The one who stays at the shore all night
And comes back with her pearls glowing white.

There she sits upon her balcony
Staring down at the brightly coloured ground
And she walks around five times in a row
Down six passages that lead to a boat.

Turn around and see a girl -
Not an ordinary girl
But the girl with the pearl earrings
Who walks around five times in a row
Down six passages that lead to a boat.
Turn around and see a girl
But the girl with the pearl earrings.

Matilda Gunnery (9)
Wyvil Primary School

The Winter

The winter is in December
There's no way you can't remember
A special time of the year
That brings you lots of cheer.

Snow comes in winter
You might get a great big splinter
The winter is cold but it can be solved
It's fun to play with but it's hard to hate it
And that's the way the winter flows.

Alice Vilanculo (10)
Wyvil Primary School

My Mum

My mum can do anything for me.
She tucks me in at night,
She hugs me very tight.
My mum cooks my dinner,
Then I feel better
And I sleep better at night.
My mum does my hair
Every day of the year
And sometimes gives me a scare.
She sometimes gives me a cheer
And says *yeah!*
My mum is like a glow in my eyes
Shining very bright.

Sammy Jo Handley (8)
Wyvil Primary School

The Sky

The sky, the sky, the blessed sky,
As blessed as the deep blue sea.

The night, the night, the dark, dark night,
As dark as can be.

The sun, the sun, the bright, bright sun,
As bright as the sun is.

The stars, the stars, the bright yellow stars,
As yellow as yellow can be.

The moon, the moon, the big, big moon,
So big, it's big enough for all to see.

Natasha Oviri (9)
Wyvil Primary School

The Pied Piper Of London

In a city called London, long ago,
There was an incalculable problem that I do know.
The problem was rats, rats here, rats there,
They fought the cats, it wasn't fair.
The noise rats made, people wouldn't admire,
For the squeaking and the shrieking, it sounded like a choir.

Now the mayor, I mean the Prime Minister, Tony Blair,
With a great big palace and nearly no hair,
He started thinking (for the very first time),
But he doesn't have a brain better than mine.
Suddenly came in a strange-looking man,
'I can solve the problem, I can, I can.'
So Tony Blair, feeling kind,
Said he could, that he wouldn't mind.
So they shook hands, for a deal
Of thousands, maybe a meal.

The very next day the rats were taken away,
Vanished! Gone! Gone!
The people cheered (that's all I can say),
For what the pied piper had done!

The people were running through the town
And trust me, the Prime Minister had a big frown.
For now he had a thousand dollars to pay,
He said he would promise, oh yes he did say.
But when the pied piper quickly came back,
There was no sack of money, no sack! No sack!

So the pied piper, really looking sad,
Thought, because of that, he would become bad!
Playing a tune, on his flute,
He took all the children away
And believe it or not,
They were all gone by the end of the day.

And now the town is sad,
Because of the Prime Minister (he's bad),
But they never forget the children,
The lassies and the lads.

Sara Andrade (10)
Wyvil Primary School

Scared

Scared of dogs
Scared of frogs
Scared of teachers
Scared of lemurs
Scared of bats
Scared of cats
Scared of fishes
Scared of witches
Scared of cheetahs
Scared of meteors.

Daniel Ferreira (8)
Wyvil Primary School

Sea Animals

I went to the polar lands and what did I see?
Porpoises and fishes that played with me.
I went to the beach and what did I see?
Starfish and seagulls that sang to the sea.
I went down under and what did I see?
People who swam and raced with me.

Jermaine Elor (8)
Wyvil Primary School

Love

Love is what you give or receive,
But doesn't come from the bin.
Love comes from the heart,
Just like the spirits from above.

Love is a treasure
That you can keep forever,
'Cause love is something if you give it away,
You end up having more.

Kennedy Mwangi (10)
Wyvil Primary School

Friends

Friends are like puzzles which fix together.
To have a friend you will have to be very
Passionate, kind and considerate.
A true friend would say you make them smile,
Even on the worst day.
You are as sweet as sugar and you are part of my life.
Losing you would be like losing a part of my life.
I will never forget you.

Precious Ogbonna (10)
Wyvil Primary School

Bingo

Adults like bingo,
It is like a yo-yo,
It's famous in some countries
But isn't played in others.

Bingo is challenging like the world is banging.
Bingo is a competition where lots of people enter,
To write some numbers and get them all right and
Win some money to go on cruises.

Jordan James (10)
Wyvil Primary School

50 Cent

50 Cent is cool,
50 Cent rules,
50 Cent makes people look like fools.

50 Cent has a car,
50 Cent hates Ja Rule,
other rap stars can't test the best
and that is 50 Cent.

Tyron Oyemade (9)
Wyvil Primary School

My Idol

My idol is Ja Rule,
No one else can test him.
He's the best of the rest,
Because he has to be the best.
Sometimes he makes me mad with his songs,
But he's still my idol.
But it would be better if he was like Fifty,
No way, he's my idol.

Ejiro Akpoveta (10)
Wyvil Primary School

I Like . . .

I like ice cream
I like football
I like maths
I like computers
I like sunshine
I like playing
I like Hula Hoops
I like lunchtime
I like being me.

Ishmael Daley (9)
Wyvil Primary School

My Valentine

You're my favourite valentine,
I love you very much,
I love you even better,
Than the world's most special dove.

You're my favourite valentine,
And that's true for sure,
Your love is like a treasure,
That I can keep for evermore.

I love you forever,
Forever you rule,
You gave me your love
And forever be true.

Fatou Jobe (11)
Wyvil Primary School

The Night Stars

The night stars are like a golden Rolex,
They shine in the sky, nice, bright and beautiful.
The night stars are like balloons, they float and stay in the sky.
The night stars are like fairies, they make your wishes come true.

If it wasn't for the night stars, night would not be night.
If it wasn't for the night stars, the sun wouldn't unlock herself
For it to be a beautiful day.

The night stars are like a golden Rolex, balloon and fairy,
If it wasn't for the night stars, night wouldn't be night
And the sun couldn't unlock herself.

Daniel Hurd (9)
Wyvil Primary School

It Would Be Obscene

It would be obscene
If the Queen turned green
It would be much more patriotic
To turn red, white and blue.

It is silly
It will be funny
Green! Not a suitable
Colour to be.

It would be obscene
If the Queen turned green
It would be much more patriotic
To turn red, white and blue.

Liliana Duarte (10)
Wyvil Primary School

Swordfish

Swordfish, swordfish, eat the jelly
Swordfish, swordfish, you're very bad
Swordfish, swordfish, don't show yourself
Swordfish, swordfish, don't get upset
Swordfish, swordfish, go to land
Swordfish, swordfish, you are lucky
Swordfish, swordfish, you aren't bad
Swordfish, swordfish, you are bright
Swordfish, swordfish, eat your pie
Swordfish, swordfish, you are home
Swordfish, swordfish, go to bed
Swordfish, swordfish, eat your bread.

Fabio Rodrigues (8)
Wyvil Primary School

Best Kinds Of People

My idol is my cousin,
Her name is Stephanie Esson.
I love her so, she knows my flow
And her favourite Teletubbie is Po.

A good singer is my mum,
She is not very dumb.
I love her so, she knows my flow
And her favourite song is 'Go! Go! Go!'

My best friend is Rhianna Spencer
If I get angry with her, I try to get calm
I love her so, she knows my flow
And her favourite cake is chocolate gâteau.

A good friend is called Ebony,
She doesn't like a boy called Kennedy,
I love her so, she knows my flow
And her most liked dance is 'Heel and Toe'.

I know a boy, he is Ejiro,
He doesn't like a boy called Pederico.
He's not a crow, he must know my flow
And he thinks he's really ghetto.

I am a girl called Sophie,
I really like to eat toffee.
I admire me so, of course I know my flow
And I love to sing . . .
Just gimme the light and pass the dough!

Sophia Thompson (9)
Wyvil Primary School

Mum

With three letters only
Mum is a small word.
It is one of the shortest
But it's biggest in the world!

Luis Gaudencio (8)
Wyvil Primary School

We're Living In A Prison

We're living in a prison,
The government says we're free,
But yet they're the ones holding the key.
The key to freedom,
The ability to express ourselves is being withheld.

We're trapped behind bars,
Being told what to do,
Will we ever be free?

How did we get time?
What time is it really now?
As it goes past we ask ourselves,
Is this reality or is this the matrix?

But the real question is, will we ever know?

Jodeci Rowe-Matthews (11)
Wyvil Primary School

The Weather

The beach, the beach, the beach, summer bay
Wouldn't it be a nice day to go out and play?
The rain, the rain, the twinkling rain,
Why do I always get the blame?
The cloud, the cloud, the cloudy sky,
When my daughter looks at it, she wants to cry.
The wind, the wind, the heavy wind,
We hope that guides us even in spring.
The snow, the snow, a snowy day,
If you stay inside you will be OK.
The rainbow, the rainbow, the colourful rainbow,
If I didn't see it, it would be pretty shameful.

Hayden Morrison (8)
Wyvil Primary School

My Skipping Poem

Skip! Skip! On the way
We will go to the park and play.
Skip in the park, people will see
You skip and jump and hurt your knee.
Mum will come and stick a plaster
Your knee will feel better.
So skip! Skip on the way
To home we will stay.

Raheema Abdirizaq (8)
Wyvil Primary School

Football

F is for football
O is for offside
O is for off target
T is for two yellow cards
B is for ball
A is for all the fans
L is for lovely footwork
L is for looking good.

Rasak Obanigba (9)
Wyvil Primary School

My Poem

M is for Mum
Y is for young

P is for people
O is for obey
E is for everyone
M is for magical.

Asia Vassel (8)
Wyvil Primary School

Flower Poem

Flowers are great, flowers are pale,
Flowers are fun, flowers don't smell,
Flowers are yellow, flowers are blue,
Flowers are nice, they're always there for you.
Flowers make you dizzy, flowers make you sneeze,
Flowers make your eyes itch, flowers attract bees,
Flowers can be sold, flowers can make money,
Flowers are useful, flowers can make honey.
Flowers aren't always small, flowers can be trees,
But most of all, flowers can make you at ease.

Ibilola Macaulay (10)
Wyvil Primary School

The Sea Poem

The sea can be blue
The sea can be glue
The sea can be red
As a shining ted.
The sea can be blue
The sea can be green
As a sea I've ever seen.
The sea can be a belly
The sea can turn into a jelly.

Marcio Pereira (8)
Wyvil Primary School

I Saw . . .

I saw an ant in a pie
I saw a bird fly up high
I saw a cat like a dog
I saw a puppy playing with a frog
I saw a spider eat a fly
I saw an ox saying bye
I saw a horse walk a mile
I saw a pony make a file
I saw a mouse in my tray
I saw a pigeon made of clay
I saw three men who saw these too
And will confirm what I tell you.

Gustavo Honorato (9)
Wyvil Primary School

Scared Of . . .

I'm scared of dirty rats
I'm scared of ugly bats
I'm scared of stinky cats
Go away you silly spats

I'm scared of gigantic stars
I'm scared of smelly Mars
I'm scared of big bars
Shoo, shoo, you silly old chocolate.

Elisabete Fernandes (9)
Wyvil Primary School